FINDING PURPOSE AT WORK

DAVIN SALVAGNO

FOREWORD BY KEN BLANCHARD

DEDICATION

To my bride, Amy, who was a writer long before I was. Thank you for putting up with my long trips away, my sleepless nights at home, my relentless use of commas, and my borderline obnoxious positivity. Thank you for always believing in me, supporting me, and loving me, even in my worst moments; for sacrificing so much of yourself for our family over the years; and for always being a physical reminder of the indescribable gift of grace that I have been given.

To my kiddos, Vera and Bennett, I pray that my words in these pages will guide you as you grow older, that they will help you discover and hold true to who God called you to be, so that you can make the impact in this life that He created you for.

CONTENTS

WITH GRATITUDE

To Ken Blanchard, for modeling what servant leadership looks like, for a lifetime dedicated to helping others identify the leader within themselves, for shaping me as a leader, and for inspiring me to finish this work.

To John C. Maxwell, for equipping me to understand more deeply the concepts of leadership through your many works, for helping me find the leader within myself, and for reassuring me that it is okay to fail as long as we fail forward.

To Patrick Lencioni, for guiding me through your work over the years to understand team dynamics and what true organizational health looks like, helping me to become a better leader for others.

To Simon Sinek, for bringing back into the spotlight the most important question we could ask: Why, a foundational element of finding purpose, and for serving as a spotlight for so many other thought leaders and igniters through your work.

To Bob Buford, for flipping my journey upside down with your book Halftime, shifting my mindset to pursue significance over success, and keeping me focused on "What's in the box."

To Brene' Brown, for unleashing the power of vulnerability, for challenging each of us to be our most authentic selves, for daring us to lead, and to do so greatly.

To Randy Tomko, for being not just a pastor but a friend and mentor over the years, keeping my eyes fixed on the only thing that matters when it's all been said and done, for modeling what it looks like to lead from the heart, and for challenging me many years ago to not let that piece of me that cares most for people die to pursue personal gain.

To Brad Seitzinger, for never giving up on me, for believing in me, for consistently challenging me, for supporting me, and for helping me become a better coach of others, but most of all for your true friendship and fellowship over the years.

To Kurt David, for taking a chance on a newfound friend's dream, for believing in the vision that I was given, for keeping me focused and reeled in over the years, for not letting me give up, for challenging me to think differently when I needed to, and for being a great business partner and friend.

To Joe Sciacchitano, for being the friend who sticks closer than a brother through my many transitions in life. From the very beginning of this journey of purpose, you believed in me and in this vision and have served selflessly at all hours of the day and night as a sounding board, a resource to our organization, and a critical member of our team. Most importantly, you have always put our friendship before anything else.

To David Smith, for being a friend and confidant over the years, for introducing me to Bob Buford's work, and for believing in me when I didn't believe in myself.

To Brian Wassom, for being a voice of wise counsel and perspective in my life and along this journey. For your constant support, encouragement, and friendship.

To Dwight Eberts, for countless conversations over the years that have led to critical and meaningful decisions along this journey, for believing in this work that was set upon my heart, for giving me opportunities to serve others, and mostly for your unconditional support, your many prayers, and cherished friendship.

To Dennis Moseley-Williams, for our rich, long-distance conversations over the years, many on airplanes or in hotel rooms as we passed as ships in the night, to share our gift of inspiration and insights with the world.

To Roger Norberg, for introducing me to the C12 Group and giving me the opportunity to join such an incredible fellowship of leaders, for bringing Kurt David and I together and for believing in our vision, for finding opportunities to support us along each step of our journey, and above all for your friendship, fellowship, and servant leadership.

To the members of the PurposePoint team, for your relentless and selfless pursuit of engaging, inspiring, and impacting the lives of others, and to the clients we have served over the years who have invited us to engage their purpose and their people.

To my parents, who have always believed in me, supported me, and encouraged me through the challenges and changes we have gone through together, for being there for me in times when I needed them, and for cheering me on along this journey.

To Steven Valtri, my uncle, who has always been the big brother I never had, for believing in me, supporting me, and inspiring me to achieve something of significance in this life without sacrificing my values or losing sight of the things that truly matter.

And finally to my grandparents, who are no longer around to read this, but who shaped me at an early age, imprinting values on my heart that have guided every decision I have made in this life, who modeled for me what living an others–focused life looks like, and for giving me a vision of the kind of person I wanted to become, and am still becoming.

FOREWORD

When Davin Salvagno first told me about his upcoming book, *Finding Purpose at Work*, I was so intrigued I immediately offered to write the foreword. Why? Because I believe that what Davin has to say is important, and that people need to hear it.

I have been a big believer in the power of purpose for a long time. To me, without a clear sense of who we are, where we are going, and the values that will guide our journey, we could be open to all kinds of distractions and our lives could get out of control. Having a clear purpose helps us use our time to the best advantage by knowing how we want to show up in the world and where we want to focus.

This was important for me to learn, because I tend to say yes too often. I am a positive-thinking guy, so lots of ideas sound good to me. But I had to realize I couldn't do it all. So with some help from Jesse Lyn Stoner, my coauthor on the book *Full Steam Ahead! Unleash the Power of Vision in Your Work and Your Life*, I created my personal vision statement. It reads: "I am a loving teacher and example of simple truths who helps and motivates myself and others to awaken the presence of God in our lives and to realize that we are here to serve, not to be served." Every morning I read this statement as one of my daily affirmations to renew my focus on who I am, where I am going, and why.

Davin and I share the belief that finding purpose at work is all-important. When an individual, a team, or an organization has clarity of purpose, they can step forward with confidence knowing they are moving in a positive direction toward their goals.

As you read about Davin's twenty-year journey toward purpose, you'll become acquainted with the people and ideas that have shaped both his thinking on the power of purpose and his decision to share his passion with others. Davin's most sincere desire is to help you, the reader, realize the same satisfaction he has achieved as you do the work to discover your own purpose and that of your organization. *Finding Purpose at Work* is the blueprint that will guide you.

Thanks, Davin, for sharing your life in a way that will help us live the rest of our lives with purpose as we strive to make a positive difference in the world.

—Ken Blanchard, coauthor of *The New One Minute Manager*® and *Servant Leadership in Action: How You Can Achieve Great Relationships and Results*

INTRODUCTION

One can never know where their journey of purpose will lead them. In the fall of 2019, I had just wrapped up a speaking tour and was ready to retreat to Boca Roton, Florida, with the family to attend a global partners church-planting conference that would also provide some much-needed rest and reflection. However, when I landed back home in Detroit from my travels on the west coast, Amy, my bride, had come down with pneumonia and we would end up canceling the trip to Boca.

A few months later, David Nelms, Founder of the Timothy Initiative, the organization that hosted the global partners weekend we missed in Boca, reached out to invite us to a similar retreat in February of 2020 in Laguna Beach, California. I gratefully accepted the invitation. The closest airport to Laguna Beach is John Wayne (SAN), and it just so happened that I had a client in the area at the time who I contacted to advise I would be in town and to see if he would like to grab dinner. It turned out that he was hosting a client appreciation event that day and asked if I would come in early to speak at it. He also mentioned another client event in Lake Tahoe the following week and asked if I could stay to speak at that event as well. So, what started as a church-planting weekend turned into an eight-day trip, and it is actually on the return flight home from this trip that I am typing these very words.

As I built out the itinerary for these eight days, there was only one day that was clear of any commitment, and I had planned to use that day to just rest and write, until I received a phone call. Our company, PurposePoint, had become a Channel Partner of the Ken Blanchard Companies so that we could provide our clients with the best possible leadership training resources available, and we had just placed a significant order for leadership training for one of our clients. The phone call I received was from our support partner Michelle at Blanchard, inviting me to their Partners Conference in San Diego to have dinner with Ken and their team, and guess what day it was on? The one day I had clear on my itinerary. Of course, I did not hesitate to change my travel arrangements to make that happen.

The morning of the Blanchard Conference came, and I showed up with high excitement and anticipation to meet Ken that evening after twenty years of being steeped in his work, but I didn't have to wait because Ken walked in right behind me. I turned to meet the man I considered a mentor for two decades, and after a brief introduction he said, "Tell me, young man, have you had breakfast yet?"

I said, "No sir."

He gently put one are around me, while the other held his walking stick firmly, and said "Let's go get something to eat." It would be at that breakfast that the foreword you just read came to be.

The intent behind the title of this book, *Finding Purpose at Work*, may seem obvious—How do we find meaning and fulfillment in the work that we do? Even more importantly, how do we make a difference in this world through our work? I will cover those questions in great detail in the chapters ahead, but there is another meaning behind the title to follow here—finding purpose at work in our lives every day and in every moment. The story I just shared about meeting Ken on the one day I had available in my travels, and the series of events that had to fall into place prior for that to happen, is an example of what I'm talking about. Certainly none of us want to see our loved ones become ill, and we often ask ourselves the question, *What is the purpose of this?* in such times. Had Amy not come down with pneumonia, our trip to Boca in November would not have been canceled, I would have not rescheduled to California a few months later, I would have not met Ken when I did, and this book would likely still be just a bunch of pages of notes still waiting to be written. If we look at every circumstance, we can often find purpose at work in it, although not always, and we often can't see the purpose until after the moment has passed. I'm sure there is at least a moment or two where you experienced car issues and the thought that you were perhaps spared from an accident due to that delay crossed your mind. In chapter two of this book, I will share my personal journey that has led to this moment of time. The intent of sharing my story is not to talk about myself, but to expose purpose at work through different moments of my life and to encourage you to look back and find purpose at work in your own life.

I once heard a very successful, and humble leader say, "Who I am is less important than what I have to say." I would add to that, "What I have to say is less important than what you actually do with it." The purpose of putting these words to paper in the pages that follow is to call you to action. This book is not an autobiography, it's not just a book on leadership or a another self-help book, it is not meant to define your purpose for you, or to force mine upon you but rather to serve as a guide to help you to discover your own purpose as an individual or as an organization and, once you find it, to never let go.

This brief work is a compilation of a twenty-year journey of trying to figure out what I wanted to do with my life and, more importantly, what God wanted to do with my life. Regardless of where you stand in your personal journey of faith, and while this is not intended to be a faith-based book, it impossible for me to share the insight, wisdom, and stories presented here without recognizing Him. It is important to understand from the very beginning that this book and my work are not about me or anything that I have accomplished. I consider all that I am and all that I have done the work of the hands of my Creator.

It has long been said that the difference between who we are and who we will be are the books we read and the people that we listen to. I have found that to be a profound truth in my life, so much so that when I look at my very own life and who I have become, I am merely a compilation of thoughts, quotes, and lyrics from people, books, and music that have shaped me. It is difficult for me to respond when asked for my favorite book or song because there are so many that have impacted me over the years. Some of the very best are those that have simply re-stated or rephrased thoughts of those whom have gone before them. This book may prove to be very much the same, and I should only hope so. A thought came to me one day to, Choose to be the spotlight rather than to be in the spotlight. I hope that this book does just that, drawing attention not to me but to people and thoughts that have shaped me, to others whom I have shared them with, and to organizations that I have had the privilege to serve.

Before you begin, I encourage you to pause. Silence the noise around you. Take a breath. Close your eyes. Remember your younger self, sitting at a desk in school, envisioning who you wanted to become and what you want to do with your life. No matter how life has played out so far, it is never too late to find your purpose or to start a new journey. Circumstances don't define you, choices do. The fact that you are reading this book right now is proof of that. Regardless of where you have been, what you have done, or where you find yourself right now, you are choosing to read something that will better yourself and perhaps change your circumstances. It is my hope that reading this book will be one of many moments you will be able to look back on where you found purpose at work in your life.

—Davin Salvagno

CHAPTER 1:
FINDING PURPOSE

Two years ago, I sat in a diner with a good friend of mine, a well-respected and accomplished individual in his industry. He ordered his gluten-free skillet, and I my usual two by two—two eggs, bacon, toast, and potatoes. Normally we would have a relaxing conversation that typically started with something like, "So, how is the family" or "How are the kids doing?" This day would be much different, and I didn't see it coming. I was in a season of career reflection, a sort of work midlife crisis, evaluating the impact I was truly making in my career and in the lives of others, wondering if any of it really mattered. He sat and listened graciously, and then pulled out a pad of post-it notes and a pen and challenged me with some insightful questions. The next hour changed my life as I pondered the journey I had been on and the shifting landscape of the current workplace.

Go to school, get a great education, then find a strong stable company to work for, grow with, and retire with. For decades, this was the basic outline for a successful career path. I remember a time, not so long ago, during my HR years when reviewing resumes that listed three job changes in ten years would send up all sorts of red flags. In fact, any more than that would immediately disqualify your resume from my desk. In 2019, finding a candidate with just three jobs in ten years was suddenly refreshing, but sadly so. We found ourselves in uncharted territory, a time when the average American under the age of thirty had an average job life span of just two years. These once-called job hoppers were not only jumping from one company to another, they were jumping from one industry to another, many of them for less pay. In fact, a 2019 Gallop study showed that seventy percent of individuals who switched jobs in 2019 found a new job with less pay but more meaning.

How does one find meaning and fulfillment in their work?

The answer lies in the basic questions that we all asked ourselves long before we entered the workforce, even before we graduated secondary school.

- What do I love to do?

- What is it I am great at?

- What does the world need?

- What can I get paid to do?

What do I love to do? Every person at some time in their life has asked themselves this question. It is likely one of the questions you asked yourself when you picked up this book. Why? Because we have been searching for answers since the beginning of time. What is the meaning of life? Why are we here? Why am I here? What is my purpose?

Because we are innately self-centered creatures, it is only natural to assume that finding the answer to our purpose begins with seeking that which fulfills us, but that is not where the journey of identifying purpose begins.

If today you became an inventor and you could create anything, what would it be? Where would you start? What questions would you ask yourself? Regardless of your why, which we will get to later on in this book, the first questions you are likely to ask is "What do people need, or what can they use?" The next question you are likely to ask is, "Has that been created yet?" If it has not, the next question will be "Can I create it, and how?" Notice the starting point of this process was not about the invention, it was about the people who would find value in its creation and the purpose it would serve.

You were created with a unique purpose, one that has immense value, and that value is determined by the value your purpose adds to the lives of others. This is where the journey of finding purpose starts, not with ourselves but with others. This is also why, for generations, this question had remained unanswered for many because our natural instinct is not to think about others but to think about ourselves.

So, to make this journey feel natural, let's start there. Let's start with the following questions: What am I great at? What are my God-given gifts, talents, and abilities?

Well, to answer that you have to place value on whatever those gifts are and where that value is found. That value is determined by how your gifts and abilities benefit others.

You might be the best underwater basket weaver on the planet, but guess what, people don't need it. There is no value there.

You see, we are back to starting with others. So, let's combine those two questions and start here …

What is it that I am great at that other people need?

This is the starting point of finding individual purpose. Some of you might already be asking, "Isn't loving what I do important?" Yes, it is, but it is only part of what makes up your purpose.

The Elements of Purpose

The same four questions I mentioned earlier are the four elements of purpose:

- What do I love to do?

- What am I great at?

- What does the world need?

- What can I get paid to do?

It has widely been accepted that there are four elements of purpose, which have been illustrated in many variations of a simple Venn diagram. Some versions of this diagram have the word Ikigai in the center, which is a Japanese concept meaning a reason for being, but the elements remain the same.

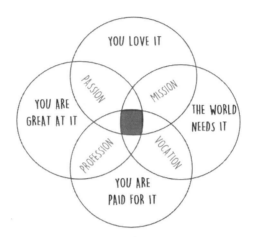

Most people start their journey of identifying their purpose by asking "How can I get paid to do what I love to do?" Do you remember the old saying, "If you do what you love, you will never work a day in your life?" There is some truth in this statement. The challenge is that work is an essential part of who we are, of personal and professional development, of self-fulfillment; it is a platform for us to express and utilize our gifts.

John Wooden is considered the greatest NCAA basketball head coach of all time. But many people knew him simply as coach, and for good reason. On the court, Wooden led the UCLA Bruins men's basketball program to an impressive number of wins, with a 664-162 record, and was named the NCAA College Basketball Coach of the Year six times. In his more than forty years as a coach, Wooden built teams, an elite athletic program, and a legacy that captivated the sports world. While his success on the court is widely known and celebrated, Wooden's impact extends far beyond sports. He had a gift as a master teacher. He taught his students that academic success was about more than grades, and he taught his players that a victory was about more than the number on the scoreboard. He cared deeply for the athletes. He taught them to be winners, not just on the court but also in life. He inspired his students and players to work their hardest, to become the very best versions of themselves.

I'm certain that if we had the opportunity to ask Wooden if coaching and teaching was his purpose in this life, he would say yes, not because he loved doing it and got paid to do so, but because he was good at it and his gifts met the needs of those around him. That is what he fell in love with, the impact of helping his players become the best they could be in every aspect of life.

Equally, if not more important than what we do, is how we do it. Wooden's legacy is not just his record or list of accomplishments, but who he was. He knew where his gifts came from, and had a good sense of self-awareness. He often said, "Talent is God given. Be humble. Fame is man-given. Be grateful. Conceit is self-given. Be careful."

Reflecting on impactful lives like Wooden's, a more chronological outline to purpose might look like this:

1. What is it that I am great at?

2. How can I help others by doing that?

3. If I spent my life doing that, would I continue to love it?

4. Is that something that I can get paid to do?

It's important to note that what you can get paid to do is last on this list for a reason. As an individual, we can have many purposes, some more important than others, and those are the ones we often do not get paid for. A few years ago, a video clip of a job interview went viral. Here is an excerpt from that clip:

"Let me tell you a little bit about the job to get started with. It's not just a job, it's sort of, probably the most important job. The title that we have going right now is director of operations, but it's really kind of so much more than that. Responsibilities and requirements are really quite extensive. First category for the requirements would be mobility. This job requires that you must be able to work standing up most or really all of the time. Constantly on your feet, constantly bending over, constantly exerting yourself for a high level of stamina. This position requires excellent negotiation and inter-personal skills. We are really looking for someone that might have a degree in medicine, in finance, and the culinary arts. You must be able to wear several hats. Associate needs constant attention. Sometimes they have to stay up with an associate throughout the night. Being able to work in a chaotic environment. If you had a life, we'd ask you to sort of give that life up. No vacations. In fact, Thanksgiving, Christmas, New Year's and holidays the workload is going to go up. And we demand that with … with a happy disposition. The meaningful connections that you make and the feeling that you get from really helping your associate are immeasurable. Also let's cover the salary, the position is going to pay absolutely nothing."

Absurd. Who would take such a job? Yet hundreds of millions take on this job every day.

The job? A Mom.

Some of the most important jobs we will ever do have nothing to do with pay, and yet everything to do with purpose. Now, I'm not suggesting that society all of a sudden switch to a pro-bono model because that would be ridiculous, but it is important we recognize that if we are going to truly operate in the center of our purpose, compensation has to be the last factor we consider.

Life Experiences

Another important aspect of our purpose not on this list is our experiences. Our experiences are powerful, for they shape our beliefs, which shape our thoughts, which then shape our behaviors and actions. Sometimes how we share our experiences with others has the same ripple effect, and those experiences are then called insights. Sean Delaney's results cone illustrates it as seen here.

We can see clearly how purpose can influence results in our lives and in our organizations. Sometimes we awaken others to their own purpose by sharing our experiences with them or providing them with insights. In the very act of doing so, we may be fulfilling our own purpose in that very moment. I can list countless conversations and moments in which the end result of the meeting was positively different from its initial intended purpose. I'm sure you can look back at your own life and see moments and conversations that have shaped how you think, what you have done, and who you are today.

Each of our lives is a journey that is continually shaped by the questions we ask ourselves, by the experiences we encounter, the insights we gain from those around us, by how we think, what we believe to be true, by the decisions we make, the behaviors we exhibit, the actions we take, and the results of those actions.

The most important question we must ask ourselves each day in the midst of that journey is, *Am I operating in my purpose?*

As Jim Collins, author of *From Good to Great* once said, *"We only get one life, and the urgency of getting on with what we are meant to do increases every day. The clock is ticking."*

While this is not intended to be an autobiography by any means, I believe it is important to share an overview of my journey with you in this next chapter, and how that journey led to my purpose and this book.

As Brene' Brown, whom I greatly appreciate for giving a voice to vulnerability in a time when we all so desperately needed it said, "When we have the courage to walk into our story and own it, we get to write the ending."

As we take a walk through a bit of my story, I encourage you to reflect on yours, specifically on the chain of events in your life and the choices you have made that have led you to where you are today.

Throughout the remainder of this book, I encourage you to also think about the lives you have already affected along your journey and, if you consider yourself a leader, which we will talk much about, I implore you to think about who it is you are helping those around you become. For it is within the affect we have on the lives of others that we find our purpose.

CHAPTER 2:
THE ROAD
LESS TRAVELED

Our natural tendency is to compare our journeys, especially in the age of social media. We size each other up, we compare ourselves to one another based on a lie others may be living, the positions we see them in, and the destinations that life takes them to. Rarely do we take the time to consider the road they traveled, the adversity they may have faced, and the decisions they had to make along the way. As a popular Chick-fil-A commercial illustrates, "Everyone has a story ... if we bother to read it." This is mine.

Humble Beginnings

When I was born in 1980, my parents lived in a one-bedroom apartment; they turned their bedroom closet into my bedroom. We were what some would call poor, although having traveled to third world countries I hesitate to describe our life as such. It was a simple and humble beginning that I have always looked back on as a benchmark to remain grateful for the many blessings we have today, even in the hardest of circumstances.

In 1984 my sister was born and, sadly, just one year later, my parents divorced. I moved in with my grandparents at the age of five, where they raised me for the next three years, while my younger sister stayed with my mother in North Philly. A few years later, our parents both re-married, which today might seem like the norm, but adjusting as a five-year-old to two sets of parents in the mid 1980s was more than difficult. Today I am grateful for all of them.

I left my grandparents' home and moved to North Philly with my mother and sister in 1988, into a home with barred windows. It was by no means a good neighborhood, but it was what my parents could provide at the time. I remember very vividly walking to school one day and being struck in the head with a baseball bat for refusing to buy drugs at just eight years of age. I can still remember the feeling of that moment whenever I touch that soft spot on my head. That was a wake-up call for my parents, so back to South Philly with my grandparents I went.

In 1992, we moved once again from my hometown of Philly across the Delaware River to Delran, New Jersey, and my sister and I alternated time with my parents between the two cities on the weekends. This was the first big change for me, outside of my parents' divorce, as I had always been a city boy, a Philly boy, and now I was living in the suburbs in New Jersey. The only real reason we ever went to Jersey was to get gas because it was cheaper, and to go to the shore during summer weekends, which to this day are some of the warmest memories of my childhood.

World Upended

In 1997, my world flipped upside down. We moved my senior year of high school much further away, from the familiarity of the Greater Philadelphia Area and the East Coast, into the unknown of Michigan and the Midwest. I was pulled away from a class of 119 students, who I had grown in relationship with over the last five years, into a senior class of 729 students, who out of my bitterness and rebellion I had no interest in making friends with. I was more than alone, and I reacted poorly. My GPA severely suffered and instead of going to Penn State, I attended Macomb Community College upon graduation in 1998.

In 2002, I dropped out during my junior year of college, while working as a cashier at Costco, to take a job as a marketing manager with Costco. I had no marketing experience or education. Yes, you read that right, no marketing experience or education. The job paid more than double the teacher's salary I would have earned, once I graduated and if I found a teaching job, which was not a certainty at the time. I was passionate about educating people, even if it was simply about the benefits of a Costco membership and eventually the Costco business model. I had a gift of communicating with people, which leaders in the organization noticed. Apparently for my age I was great at it, they needed it, I loved it, and they paid me to do it. This was my first encounter with operating in the center of my purpose. I quickly found myself on the fast track to success with a well-respected company, a company that exemplified what taking care of their people and their customers truly looked like, led by a CEO, Jim Sinegal, who was the walking definition of engagement. I'll share more about this experience, how his leadership shaped my journey and my purpose, later on in this book.

Defining Moments

Two short years later, 2004 proved to be the most defining year of my life. The decisions I made during this year shaped my purpose more than any other. Shortly after being promoted to marketing manager, I was offered another promotion to a larger role with Costco based in New Jersey, just ten minutes away from where we had previously lived. Life could not seem to be more perfect in this moment—the stars had aligned as some would say.

I accepted the job, and as excited as I was, something didn't feel right. You see, having been born into a one hundred percent Italian home, I was naturally raised Catholic, but I was distant from God, holding onto the bitterness from my childhood circumstances. Earlier that year, I had seen *The Passion of The Christ*, and it shook me to my core. I had so many questions and really started digging into what it is I believed to be true, an element of purpose that I referenced in chapter one. That year I also started working out with a personal trainer at Lifetime Fitness who was helping me train for a very competitive ice hockey tournament in Canada. Hockey had always been my sport, and while I was good at it and loved it, I was not great at it or built to play at the NHL level, so it was not my purpose as much as I wanted it to be. My personal trainer, Brian, quickly become one of my closest friends. Brian helped me get in the best shape of my life, both physically and spiritually.

That year I also attended a leadership conference with Brian and a church service that same weekend where I made the choice to accept Christ into my life. The date was January 11, 2004. Wherever you are on your journey or whatever you believe, I am in no way pushing my beliefs on you, but to not share this part of my story would compromise the entire foundation of discovering my purpose and everything that has happened in my life since. I returned from the conference that weekend and felt that God was calling me to decline the opportunity I had just accepted in New Jersey. *What? But this was perfect, wasn't it? It was everything that I had ever wanted, or was it?* It was as if I heard this small, still voice in my head saying, "Davin, if you want to return to your Philly roots and be successful with Costco, I have opened that door for you, but if you are willing to give that back to me, to trust me and stay here in Michigan, I have something so much more for you." And so, I stayed. I walked into the office the next day, rejected the job offer, and told my leaders point blank that I felt God had something more for me here. You can imagine the looks on their faces. They strongly urged me to reconsider, but I stayed the course, and I'm glad that I did.

Three days later, I received a call from my mother asking if I could take our family friend Olga to her church to attend their midweek evening service, as her husband George had to work that evening. I gladly agreed to help and attended church with her that evening. Fun fact—I love music and have played the piano since I was seven, though not very well. As a kid, I often snuck into the sanctuary of my grandparents' church in hopes that the piano was unlocked, and I played in quiet solitude as an outlet. That evening at Olga's church, I was captivated by their piano player,

Colin, who led the worship team. They played the same songs I had just heard at the service in Greensboro, North Carolina, at the leadership conference I had a attended just a few days earlier. I asked Olga if they had an affiliate church in North Carolina and they did not. Then Randy, their pastor, who simply preferred to be called by his first name, came out and gave the same message I had heard just a few days earlier. God had my complete and undivided attention.

The next morning, while sitting in my office at Costco, I received a call to come to the membership desk to take care of an issue one of our business accounts had. I walked out of my office and towards the front of the building, and there at the desk I see a familiar face … Colin, the worship leader from the night before at Rockpointe Community Church. It was the church's membership that had the issue. In excitement, I shouted unprofessionally at him "Dude, your band is awesome!" In his British accent he responded, "My band, what are you talking about?" I clearly didn't understand the dynamics of a voluntary worship band. I proceeded to tell him my story from the night before, which led to us having lunch in the food court of Costco for an hour. To this day, I don't even remember what the membership issue was or if we ever solved it!

That week I started attending Rockpointe Community Church regularly, and it was there just one year later that I met my bride, Amy, in a small group. As I write this, that was fifteen years ago, and today we are blessed with two wonderful children and an incredible community of friends, some of whom I expressed my sincere gratitude to in the beginning pages of this book.

My time at Costco came to an end in 2007. I was recruited by Macy's into a general manager (GM) role for their foods division, again with no prior GM experience, the result of a locker room conversation one day while playing hockey with the vice president of Macy's. The discussion stemmed from a passing comment I made about developing people through the alignment of individual and organizational purpose.

One year later the recession of 2008 hit, and Macy's found themselves in very challenging times. I had spent a lot of time talking about people, purpose alignment, and culture, and was asked to step into a role on the retail side to partner with operations and human resources to drive employee engagement and growth during a dark time in retail. I remember our customer survey at the time had a five-point rating scale, with the highest rating being Outstanding. This is where my psychology classes in college served me well. As I walked store floors, I asked employees how they were doing, listened intently to their responses, and when they asked me how I was doing, I always responded "Outstanding," even when I wasn't. It was a different time, a time when being vulnerable as a leader was not accepted or encouraged, as it was seen as a sign of weakness. While I wasn't being sincere in my response, I was being purposeful. My goal was to create a consistently positive culture that kept employees engaged during the worst of times and help keep them positive for our customers. I was soon given the name Captain Outstanding, and one year was presented with a cape with the Macy's star on it to wear as I visited different departments. Despite my efforts, Macy's had to make some tough decisions in the years ahead, releasing a large portion of their workforce. While my job wasn't eliminated at the time, I found myself in an environment where the purpose of my role had shifted, and my job was no longer in alignment with my individual purpose.

In 2010 I was recruited by a local international market to leave Macy's and become their GM, with future partnership potential. Eight months into that role, I was fired for the first and only time in my life. I was asked by ownership to divide their workforce into two groups, fire half of them, and replace them with better talent. That was their plan for growth. It's safe to say we did not share the same ideology of developing people and managing performance.

Connecting Purpose, People, and Process

Fortunately, CVS Health was in the process of recruiting me for a multi-unit leadership role, and I gladly accepted. I stepped into a district operations role for them, during a time where they were growing quickly through acquisition. CVS had traditionally been an organization that prided itself on execution, but was trying to figure out how to become more people oriented. The senior leaders of the organization at the time were notorious for saying, "Everything comes down to either process or people." They had process down, but they were really struggling with the people side of that statement. They even launched an enterprise-wide unfreezing session to introduce the power of the *and*—how to make it not about process *or* people, but rather process *and* people, and how to bring the two together. For me the answer was simple: Purpose. Everything comes down to purpose.

I began to transition from my district operations role at CVS Health into an HR business partner role, without an HR degree or any prior HR certifications. It was an unpopular choice to move from operations into HR, but I saw this as an opportunity to help the organization bridge the gap between the two, align the workforce around their purpose, increase engagement, reduce turnover, and ultimately improve performance. I found purpose in my work once again, and again found myself operating in the center of my purpose. As the company had nearly doubled in size since I came on board in 2010, travel increased significantly and I was asked several times to relocate my family to become an HR director for a then-Fortune 8 company. What an incredible opportunity at the age of thirty-six! But great opportunities often come at a great cost. I knew what this role meant, it meant getting on a plane on Monday and coming home on Friday, every week. We had a five and a one-year-old at home, my in-laws lived just three minutes and thirty-six seconds away from our house (which I often joke is way too close), our kids at the time were their only grandchildren, and we had become very involved with our church community. The answer for us was a hard no to relocation. I was not ready to put my children or my family through what I had gone through as a child. My purpose as a husband and father was more important than my role at CVS.

For the next year I stayed in a hybrid role and traveled occasionally. In May of 2016 I felt the call to "Take the great leap," as my friend Dennis Moseley-Williams would say. I decided to leave my role with CVS to start a consulting firm to help organizations stay connected to their purpose and to their people. I surrendered my generous salary and my stock options, leaped out on faith, and decided we would live off of our savings with a stay-at-home wife and two young children. I processed that decision with the guidance of several friends and advisors, in particular my friend Brad Seitzinger who was the managing partner of Northwestern Mutual, the financial firm that I was a client of. A by-product of that conversation landed me in a contracted growth and development director role in financial services, with no financial services education, designations, or experience. I'll expand more on that conversation in the next chapter.

In 2017, I delivered my first public speaking engagement on the topic of leading people through purpose at Northwestern Mutual to a group of community leaders. In that talk, I made this statement: "As every organization begins, they start with a purpose, they invite people to join them in that purpose, they put processes in place to support their people, and they start turning a profit. As organizations get larger and older, they tend to start focusing more on process and profit than they do on people or purpose and they start to experience inconsistency. The key to consistent sustainable growth is remembering the Purpose–Point of why you started in the first place and keeping that in front of your team at all times." And the term PurposePoint was born. I began to deliver this talk for several organizations and launched the consulting company that I had envisioned years earlier.

In 2018 I founded PurposePoint, in partnership with Kurt David and a private investor, and became an ambassador member of the C12 Group. The C12 Group provided me the opportunity to work with CEOs of organizations large and small from across the country, and the topic of popular discussion was, you guessed it, purpose. Their motto is "Building Great Businesses for a Greater Purpose." In the months to follow, PurposePoint grew to become more than a consulting organization. Other speakers from across the country who shared a similar purpose and vision asked to come alongside of our work. It was clear to me that PurposePoint was never meant to be mine but a platform for likeminded speakers, coaches, consultants, and leadership trainers to come together and collaborate, engage, inspire, and impact others, and to help organizations stay connected to their purpose and to their people.

In 2019 while sitting in a lunch session with our team, we were struck with an epiphany. We had been taking the conversation of purpose to organizations, but why not invite organizations to the conversation of purpose? We decided to host a two-day event focused on aligning individual purpose and organizational purpose and called it Purpose Summit 2019. We had four months to plan this event, did no advertising other than some grass-roots social media posts, and held it in a repurposed hundred-year-old school building in a blighted neighborhood in Detroit. We chose this location to support and draw attention to the purposeful work of LifeRemodeled, who had repurposed the building. More than 300 people showed up for the two-day conversation, and it was absolutely transformational. I was so very proud of our team, and grateful for how well they came together to transform the lives of so many individuals and organizations. Shortly thereafter, planning began for Purpose Summit 2020.

I was also honored in 2019 to be named as one of Oakland County's 40 Under 40, was appointed chair of Economic Workforce Development for the Auburn Hills Chamber of Commerce, and spoke in more than a dozen cities across the country on the concept of communicating and leading through purpose. It was on the flights traveling to and from these talks that I began work on this book.

This road has been far from traditional and far from easy, but absolutely worth it. If there is one thing I have learned along the way, it's that your circumstances don't define you. Your choices do. As Robert Frost wrote: "Two roads diverged in a wood, and I— I took the one less traveled by, and that has made all the difference."

Choose the road less traveled. Choose the road that consistently leads you to operate from the center of your purpose and that helps others find their purpose along the journey.

CHAPTER 3:
WHO ARE YOU HELPING OTHERS BECOME?

I have always wanted to be a teacher, not for the summers off, and certainly not for the pay, but for the impact. As I mentioned earlier, at the young age of five I went to live with my grandparents. While living with them, I attended a private school. As my parents were figuring out their individual journeys, I found myself being influenced by my grandparents and by my teachers. The way that I viewed my teachers and the role they played in my life had a significant impact on who I was becoming. I knew then that this was the impact I wanted to have on others as I grew up. I wanted to become a teacher so that I could play a small role in helping others become who they were created to be.

For those of you familiar with Markus Buckingham, his work revealed that others mostly see me as a teacher and a stimulator. It turned out that I became a teacher after all. The question now was, to whom and what?

Whom was I meant to teach? What was I supposed to teach them?

I felt strongly that the *who* were leaders who had a passion for people and a hunger for purpose, and the *what* were my insights from the diverse experience and the library of knowledge I had digested over the last fifteen years while climbing the corporate ladder of leadership with Costco, Macys, and CVS Health. While I built a very diverse resume over those years working in marketing, operations, and eventually human resources, it was in HR that I discovered an immense love for people and the most direct opportunity to help them become who they were created to be.

As I said in chapter one, the question we often ask ourselves is *What do I love to do?* but how often do we ask the question, *What am I good at?* Over the seven years I served in leadership at CVS Health, I asked this question often to those around me, "What is it that you think you are good at?" My mind raced to ask more questions that identified where this person could best serve in the organization and how they could better drive their performance by harnessing their talents and abilities.

During these years I rapidly digested everything there was available in this space, SLII® (Blanchard), DiSC personality styles, Strengths Finder, and so on, using all that I learned to help others become who they were created to be in every possible interaction. And yet with all that I was doing to help others become who they were created to be, rarely did I take stock of who it was that I was becoming.

We can quickly lose sight of ourselves in pursuit of success. I started to measure my accomplishments through the common HR language of improving performance rather than looking at the actual impact I was having on the lives of those I was trying to teach and lead.

When I stepped into my role at CVS in 2010, I was faced with the unique challenge of leading a newly formed team due to a recent district realignment of seventeen direct reports who had previously worked for five different district leaders just a few months earlier. They definitely operated in silos, and using Patrick Lencioni's *The Five Dysfunctions of a Team* language, there was a clear absence of trust. To make matters worse, the district leader that I was actually replacing was on leave and likely not coming back and, in her absence, the other four dysfunctions were at play as well. If you haven't read Lencioni's work, here is an illustration of the Five Dysfunctions.

I strongly recommend Lencioni's work for any leader, in particular his books *The Five Dysfunctions of a Team* and *The Advantage*.

Among the group of managers that I now found myself leading was a gentleman named Tommie. Tommie had been the acting district leader while the previous district leader was on leave before I entered the scene. Tommie was a tremendous blessing in helping me navigate through the current state of the district, introducing me to each manager, and helping me understand the dynamics of the team, (at least that's what we were supposed to be). As you can imagine though, Tommie also thought that he should have become the new district leader, after all he had basically been doing the job for the last few months. My presence obviously delayed his career progression. What I respected most about Tommie was that he was honest. He didn't hide how he felt, he came right out and told me, and I couldn't have asked for a better start to our relationship. I shared with Tommie that I knew exactly how he felt, as I had been looked over in the past, and I made a promise to him. I told him I was not there to build a name for myself, and that I would invest in him as a leader and do whatever I could to help him become who he wanted to be, who he was created to be.

Over the years that followed, Tommie supported me and I advocated for him. He was passed up a few more times, but each time we fought together, we processed the feedback he received, and we prepared him for the next opportunity. At one point, my regional leader confronted me. He said "When are you going to stop fighting for this guy? He's never going to be a district leader."

I respectfully responded, "I agree with you on many things, but not on this, you're wrong. Tommie will eventually become a district leader, and when given that chance, he will become one of the best we have."

My regional said, "What makes you so sure?"

I responded, "He's coachable, and as long as someone is coachable, there is no limit to what they can accomplish. I've seen him constantly challenge himself. He has not given up on himself, so why should we give up on him?"

Tommie eventually did become a district leader, and one of the very best.

Buy in Early on People

We look for the greatest trends in the market, the hottest start-ups, the next big idea … all in an effort to capitalize on potential. The greatest potential we can capitalize on is often right in front of us and is often overlooked.

Top performers in any industry were once beginners. CEOs of large organizations were once entry-level employees. Well-known authors and speakers were once unknown people with unspoken insights.

What if the next Jeff Bezos, Marc Benioff, Satya Nadella, or Hubert Joly were working in your organization right now? What if you recognized their potential and developed it?

What if you had access to the next Jim Collins, Ken Blanchard, Stephen Covey, Patrick Lencioni, Simon Sinek, or Brené Brown right now, before their breakout book or talk? What if you tapped into their insights?

Jeff Bezos once worked as a short-order line cook at McDonald's during the breakfast shift, as a director of customer service for a startup, and as a project manager in the banking industry, before founding Amazon in his garage on July 5, 1994.

Marc Benioff spent thirteen years in a variety of executive positions in sales, marketing, and product development before founding Salesforce in his rented San Francisco apartment in 1999.

Patrick Lencioni spent a combined ten years at Bain & Company, Oracle Corporation, and Sybase, as an employee with a liberal arts education from Claremont McKenna College, before founding The Table Group in 1997, eventually becoming one of the top CEO coaches and leadership authors of our generation.

Brené Brown began her career as a research professor at the University of Houston Graduate College of Social Work with a focus on authentic leadership and wholeheartedness in families, schools, and organizations. She presented a TED talk on *The Power of Vulnerability* in 2012, which in 2020 was one of the top five-most viewed TED talks with more than forty million views, and she also became five-time number-one *New York Times* best-selling author that year.

The next great leaders and thought leaders are among us right now. Great organizations recognize the talent within and around them, and they seize the opportunity to develop them and invest in them. The greatest opportunity to capitalize on potential, to reach our goals faster, to achieve our purpose, is right in front of us.

It's not a stock, it's not a startup, it's not a big idea. It's the people around us.

For years, business leaders have been prioritizing the wrong question: How do we increase performance?

The greatest question we must ask ourselves as leaders is: Who are we helping our people become?

An equally important follow-up question to that would be: What are we learning from them in the process?

I mentioned my friend Brad Seitzinger in the previous chapter, and promised to elaborate on the career-changing conversation we had. In May

2016, when I decided to take the great leap from my corporate role to start my own consulting company, I called Brad and asked him to lunch. For years before that, Brad had seen something in me that I had not seen in myself. We met for lunch and I shared with him that I was leaving my corporate career, that I was going to live off of stock options for a few years, and do some writing, coaching, and speaking. I laid out my plan, that I wanted to work with organizations who were passionate about their purpose and their people, and pour all that I had in me into them to help them become who they were created to be.

If you ever have an opportunity to meet Brad, you will quickly learn that he listens with an uncanny level of depth, while thinking and note-taking at the same time. After what I'm sure seemed like an eternity of me talking and him writing vigorously all over our paper tablecloth, he looked up, and said "Davin, I think you should come work here. You will find the culture you are seeking, and the opportunities you will have to help others will be endless."

Brad gave me a tremendous opportunity and introduced me to an incredible organization. While I had been a client of Northwestern Mutual for ten years, I never truly knew or appreciated what happened behind closed doors, and my words here will not do it justice. Behind those doors are people who have a level of commitment to see the lives they serve protected and provided for in ways unparalleled in their industry. They live to help others spend their lives living. They know their purpose, they lead with purpose, and they invest in their people to help them achieve their purpose. I chose to put my consulting company on hold and take Brad up on his offer. He laid out a plan for where I might best serve as a leader within the organization, and he gave me the resources and support that I needed to be successful in that role. He bought in early on me, and he went all in.

Brad and I met often, and each time we met he made me a better listener and a better coach. During one of our senior leadership sessions, which we called Capstone, I gave a presentation on how to speak with influence, and another light bulb went off. I knew in that moment that I wanted to continue to grow myself as a coach and a speaker, and then pay it forward by helping to develop other coaches and speakers. I wanted to create a ripple effect of influence. It was out of this moment that PurposePoint was born. I wanted to create an entity that focused on helping individuals and organizations become who they were created to be, to help them fulfill their purpose.

Brad and I met again for lunch and I shared my vision and, once again, he was all in. No leader wants to lose members of their team, but Brad wasn't focused on how he could use me to increase the performance of his organization, he was focused on who he was helping me become as a leader.

My time at Northwestern Mutual (NM) was short lived, just three years, but a piece of NM will always remain in me as my time there showed me what leading with purpose truly looks like. On some level, I'm sure Brad always knew that my time dedicated to NM would not last forever, yet he invested in me all the same. He chose, as a leader, to help me become who he saw that I could become, not because he was looking for return on his investment or retention, but because that's what leaders do. I will always be grateful to NM for giving me my start in this arena, and for Brad, whose focus was always on helping me to become who I was created to be.

It has long been said that people are the greatest asset of an organization. But I would offer, that people are not just the greatest asset of your organization, they are the greatest partners of your purpose, and the most important part of the organization you must steward as a leader.

Who are we helping our people become?

This is the most powerful question every leader and every organization should be asking. If you are not, you will soon be asking, *Where are our people?*

It was once overheard in this conversation:

CFO: "What if we invest in our people and they leave?"

CEO: "What if we don't and they stay?"

Sure, they may leave if you in fact help them become who they were created to be, many to eventually become leaders or CEOs of other organizations themselves. But one thing is for certain, you won't have to ask where they are, for they will likely be shining the spotlight on you because, like Brad, you helped them get there.

"Your role as a leader is even more important than you might imagine. You have the power to help people become winners."

—Ken Blanchard

A Greater Purpose

In 1998, Jason Lippert, CEO of Lippert Components, Inc. had just started up a new business unit for his family-owned and operated company, which at the time generated about seventy million dollars in revenue annually. As his leadership journey grew, so did the company, to a tune of one billion dollars in revenue in 2013. While that was a tremendous accomplishment for both him and his organization, achieving that milestone was also a transformational moment. *What comes next?* he thought. *Two billion? Three?* It was in that moment that he started seeking God's purpose for his company, and for his work as a leader. "It seems like there is so much more to life than growing a business, beating competitors, acquiring companies, developing products, and attracting new customers," Jason said. "After almost twenty years in business it seemed that I was caught up in this cycle and it didn't seem to fulfill a greater purpose outside of just bringing jobs to families." So, Jason started praying for that greater purpose to be revealed. God finally gave him an answer to those prayers in the form of a TED talk by Bob Chapman called *Truly Human Leadership*. In that twenty-minute talk, Bob emphasized that if we, as leaders, cared about people more at work, we would see employee turnover in our organizations slow down significantly. As Jason heard those words, he realized that if turnover slowed down, quality, safety, efficiency, and innovation would all get better, but what he didn't yet discover was the beginning of a much greater purpose. When he appreciated, rewarded, and respected people for the great work they were doing, it made people feel better, they trusted management more, and, most importantly, they went home happier to their families.

The work environment that Jason and his team were fostering created better family leaders. Leading families better meant parents being more intentional with their children, spouses being more aligned with each other, divorce rates in their workforce declining, and an overall greater impact on society. Additionally, as team members spent more than forty hours a week in a positive work culture that was helping them grow personally, stress levels among their team reduced significantly. Stress, it is estimated, is responsible for seventy-five percent of the chronic illnesses in our country. Creating a more caring workplace was not only reducing turnover, improving family relationships, and creating social impact, it was having a direct physical impact on the health and wellness of the each person within their organization. Once Jason and his team came to this realization, they chose to make investing in the development of their company culture their focus, because they realized that their culture is their purpose.

As I have shared before, the greatest product a company can produce is its culture. This was a transformational discovery for Jason and his team, and ultimately a new purpose point for Lippert Components, Inc (LCI). The culture journey that began at this moment of realization, and that continues today at LCI, is one of the greatest examples of purpose at work that I have found. Jason and his team started their journey with developing their core values, as most do. But developing them wasn't enough. They knew they needed to communicate those values regularly, in their evaluations, in their weekly meetings, in their daily front-line meetings. But that wasn't enough, either. They also realized that the most important thing they had to do in order to truly shape a sustainable culture was to hold their team members accountable to those values, and to do so consistently.

In the early stages of this journey, they found out that many of their people were frustrated because just having values wasn't enough, and mildly enforcing them only made people upset that they had gone to great lengths to establish great values only to not hold people accountable to those values all of the time. The values had to be non-negotiable. They had to serve as more than just a guide for how they were to work together, they had to serve as a condition to work together. Even in the most purposeful of organizations, some people are just not willing to adapt to change, and this was a big change. Jason and his team solidified the absoluteness of their new values and decided they would help people transition out of the company—some who had been with the company for ten, twenty, or thirty years—who weren't willing to change and grow.

"Leaders have to be learners and leaders in our organization have to be willing to grow. If you aren't willing to grow, by definition, other leaders will outgrow you ... more importantly, we can't accomplish our purpose impacting more and more businesses by our example if we aren't all willing to grow."

— Jason Lippert, CEO, Lippert Components

Jason and his organization continued to invest in the growth of their people. They hired a leadership coach to help teach their front-line leaders. Most of these men and women, who were leading the teams on the front-line to build products, had never had a leadership class before, let alone a leadership coach. This coach helped reiterate their core values and establish a set of leadership values that their leaders needed to embody. They soon discovered that they needed more and more leadership coaches because they had hundreds of leaders on the frontlines who didn't know the difference between leading and managing. After hiring ten leadership coaches to adequately touch the thousands of people working on their front lines, they decided they couldn't truly help grow their team members unless they had a good personal foundation. So they hired personal development coaches to implement programs such as *The Dream Achiever* modeled after the *Dream Manager* written by Matthew Kelly. I have read this book several times and have had great conversations with other leaders who have enjoyed this work, but never had I come across an organization that actually applied it so intentionally as LCI.

Jason and his team simply asked the men and women in their workforce, who self-opted into getting personal development coaching, what their dreams were and explored how they could accomplish those dreams both inside and outside of LCI. "I can't tell you how many people have uncovered dreams and cried in the process because they realized they stopped asking themselves what their dreams were when they were twelve years old. To have a business uncover this is unheard of," Jason said. They started listening sessions with the CEO and other top leaders, where Jason would travel to a plant once per week, sit down with the frontline men and women, cast the company's vision for twenty-five minutes, and then he would just sit and listen for an hour. His top-level leaders have followed his example, listening to their teams and then acting upon what they had heard. In the process, they built a level of trust they had not experienced before.

LCI had so many businesses reach out to them who had experienced what they were doing and seen how rapidly they were growing that they wanted to learn how they were doing it. So LCI started their own leadership- and culture-teaching mechanism in 2019 called The Lippert Leadership Academy. They staffed it and started teaching others what they had learned along the journey, educating those other businesses and business leaders on what needed to happen to develop a culture that has true impact and purpose to their team members. Their journey of purpose had grown beyond their walls and into their customer's places of business.

In 2020, LCI had grown to a three-billion dollar publicly traded company (LCII), and seen their employee turnover reduce from 117 percent in 2013 at the start of this journey to just 25 percent, saving them millions in turnover costs. "This journey has taught us that our purpose is to help people realize their purpose, treat our team members with love and respect as well, and give them a safe home away from home as they invest well over half of their life into their careers," Jason said. "Our goal as an organization is to invest more and more into our team members to create a great culture where we hear them say, 'I have never worked for a company that has done this for their people.' Simply put, investing personally and professionally into their lives every day. Helping them become who they were created to be."

Each of us, whether you consider yourself to be a leader or not, has the power to bring out the best in others, to help them reach their potential, to help them fulfill their purpose.

As Jim Stoval, author of *The Ultimate Gift* once said, "Who we are is a tribute to those who have left us a legacy. Who we help others become will be our legacy."

Indeed, the ultimate gift we have to give to others is helping them become who they were created to be. This is the cornerstone of our purpose, and nowhere is this more important than in roles of leadership.

CHAPTER 4:
LEADING WITH PURPOSE

"How can I help?" This is the most powerful question in the human language, and it is the calling card of any great leader. I don't watch much TV, but when I saw the trailer for the TV series *New Amsterdam* I was curious, and after watching the pilot I was hooked. The pilot opens by introducing Dr. Max Goodwin, the new medical director of New Amsterdam Hospital. Max calls an assembly of the entire hospital staff to make an introduction, and in his inaugural talk as the hospital's new leader he immediately makes a clear statement of purpose.

Max addresses the assembly and says, "Will everyone in the cardiac surgery department please raise your hands."

Hands go up.

Max looks around and then says, "You're all fired."

Looks of bewilderment and confusion cover their faces as they immediately grab their phones to start calling their attorneys.

Max continues, "Any department that places billing above patient care, you will be terminated."

We learn that the cardiology department had been abusing billing, focusing more on profitability than on their patients and their purpose.

He goes on to say, "We all want to change the system, but we are the system. So … how can I help?"

One by one Max addresses the questions and needs of what's left of his team in the assembly and leads them back to their purpose.

He engages them, inspires them, and challenges them with his closing words, "Let's be doctors again."

Every leader, every organization experiences what Peter Greer referred to as "mission drift." And this is exactly what was occurring, not only at New Amsterdam but throughout the hospital and health care system.

Peter Greer writes in his book *Mission Drift*, "In its simplest form, mission true organizations know why they exist and protect their core at all costs ... They define what is immutable: their values and purposes, their DNA, their heart and soul."

The theme throughout every episode of *New Amsterdam* is Max having to address different situations as a leader, protecting their core at all costs, making decisions that are not the profitable thing to do, as the hospital board would like, but the purposeful thing to do because that is his DNA, that is his heart and soul.

But Max is more than just a leader, he is a servant leader. In every episode Max walks into some crisis or situation that his team is facing and utters these words, "How can I help?" He consistently puts his needs second to those of his team and his patients. His selfless, bold, and often disruptive actions as a leader keep his team focused on their purpose. He is constantly reminding them of why they are there and challenging them to challenge themselves to become better, through who he is and how he leads.

Four Qualities of a Great Leader

Great leaders are accessible.

Ever since I came across *New Amsterdam*, I have found myself repeating the phrase "How can I help?" several times a day, both in my work and at home. In fact, Amy has kindly hinted more than once that she would prefer me to stop saying it, but I can't help it. These four words are the most powerful words any leader can ask, whether a spouse, parent, or CEO, because they convey a very important message: I am here, I am accessible, and you are important to me.

Great leaders are listeners.

Listening. Perhaps this is where we often fail the most as leaders. We live in such a busy time and a distracting age that it has become a challenge to be fully present in the moment and process what we are hearing. We tend to listen to respond, when we should be listening to hear. The self-discipline of listening is what sets effective leaders apart, because it leads them to ask great questions. Asking great questions is what makes leaders impactful.

Great leaders are challenging.

Good leaders ask good questions, but great leaders ask great questions. What makes a great question a great question? One that challenges us. Most people are motivated by being challenged, it is why we enjoy games, sports, and great stories. It's the challenge within each of those, rising to it, and overcoming it, that makes them great. Games that don't challenge us are boring, and stories that don't present a challenge are uninspiring. Boredom and lack of inspiration lead to inaction. It is an indisputable fact that for individuals to take action they need to be challenged, by themselves or by others who believe in their potential. The soundtracks of pivotal moments of our lives often echo great inspiring scenes from timeless movies. Imagine being on the hillside in *Braveheart* as Mel Gibson shouts "Freedom!" or huddled around Robin Williams in *Dead Poets Society* as he whispers "Carpe Diem." Whether shouting or whispering, a challenging call to action is inspiring and moves us.

A word of caution, there is a difference between being challenging and being critical. Being challenging without permission can be perceived as criticism, which then makes the leader less accessible, and ultimately not effective or impactful.

Great leaders lead with purpose.

Finally, the leader's challenge has to challenge the status quo. It must be a call to do something or become something different, and there must be a purpose worthy of the effort. It has to lead us to a place other than where we currently are. This is perhaps the most overlooked quality of leadership, because purpose comes across as a soft word, and leadership does not. Purpose is not fluff, it is foundational. Any great endeavor that has been accomplished started with a purpose, and every great leader that accomplished it kept that purpose at the forefront of their words and actions. They never lost sight of it. Purpose is not soft, it is bold and possibly begs the most challenging question each of us is faced with: What is our purpose as individuals? As organizations? As leaders?

"The key to successful leadership is influence, not authority."
—Ken Blanchard

It has often been said that leadership is simply the ability to influence. There is good influence and there is poor influence, there are good leaders and there are poor leaders.

Good leaders are often accessible and are good listeners, but shy away from being challenging.

Poor leaders are often challenging, but lack listening and accessibility.

Great leaders are both challenging and accessible. They listen, and they lead with purpose.

Situational Leadership

Situational leadership is a critical element of leading with purpose, and not all situations are created equal. We have a tendency to lead from our natural personality style. Each of us has encountered different types of leaders in our lives, and when asked to describe them, we use words like directive or supportive, we label them as delegators or coaches, and we perceive them as either a type-A or type-B personality. There are many personality assessments, such as DiSC or the Myers-Briggs Type Indicator, which can be used to determine the personality of a leader. Each type of personality can be equally effective, in the right situation. One of the most useful resources that has guided me as a leader over the years is SLII®.

I first came across SLII® in 2003 when I was introduced to *The One Minute Manager* by Ken Blanchard and Spencer Johnson. This book changed everything I knew about management and leadership, and challenged me to want to become a better leader.

In our ever-increasingly fast-paced world, we have a desire to get things done yesterday. We want results, and we want them now. Just as quickly as mission drift can happen, we can easily find ourselves directing and delegating as a leader in situations when what we really need to do is to coach and support. In your mind, you have already thought of a leader in your life and ascribed a personality style to each of those words: direct, delegate, coach, and support.

This section is not intended to be a crash course on understanding and mastering SLII®. Doing so takes time, about fifteen hours to be exact, and a lot of practice and implementation. However, it is critical to understand that if we as leaders are going to lead others with purpose, we need to be willing to invest time in them.

We need to be accessible to them and listen, we need to diagnose their confidence and competence as it relates to what we are asking them to do, and then we need to determine what type of leader they need us to be to help them to succeed.

"An effective leader must step back, look at the big picture, and make sure the important things are not being pushed out of the way by the seemingly urgent needs of the moment."

—Ken Blanchard

Too often, we sacrifice the important for the urgent. We must be very cautious to not do so, for we can easily lose sight of our people and our purpose.

Servant Leadership

Another critical element of leading with purpose is servant leadership, the act of leading and serving simultaneously. We must be clear about what servant leadership is and what it is not. Servant leadership is not always giving people what they want, it's giving people what they need. Specifically, it is giving them what they need to accomplish the purpose they are being called to. What our teams often need most from us is an impactful purpose, a motivating mission, an inspiring vision, and an uncompromising set of values.

Throughout the years, here is how I have come to define these:

Purpose—Who we are and why we exist.

Mission—What we aim to accomplish.

Vision—Where we are going.

Values—What matters most along the way.

How do purpose, mission, vision, and values relate to servant leadership? In order to ensure that these are meaningful and impactful, they must be written from an others-focused perspective, and that is the essence of servant leadership. The heart of servant leadership is being focused on others, it is a position of both authority and humility. We often have a false sense of what humility is and what it is supposed to look like. Author Timothy Keller does a tremendous job of walking us through what true humility looks like, and his book, *The Freedom of Self-Forgetfulness* sums it up nicely with this quote from C.S. Lewis, "True humility is not thinking less of one's self, it's thinking of one's self less."

This quote from Lewis is the heart of servant leadership. It's constantly taking the focus off of ourselves and placing it on those we are leading and serving.

Too many organizations have fallen into the trap of hiring a marketing company to write these statements for them and, sadly, these critical statements become nothing more than words on a wall or on a page in some employee handbook. This happens because often the focus is not placed on the people in the organization or those they are serving, but rather on what the organization wants to be known for. I'm not going to call out any organizations specifically here, but there are plenty of these statements that I could list, some from very well-known brands, that are simply marketing slogans with very little meaning.

I will expand on how to write these critical statements more effectively and give examples from organizations who do this well in a later chapter when we define the difference between purpose, mission, and why. These are three different words that have three very different meanings and implications, yet they often are used interchangeably and have become buzzwords.

Like the terms I just mentioned, servant leadership can also become a buzzword. Once introduced into a culture, these terms often become so popular so quickly that they lose their intended meaning. Purpose, mission, vision, values, and even servant leadership are more than just terms; they are words of action. It is our job as leaders to ensure that our actions and the actions of our teams are in constant alignment with the intended meaning of such words.

Take a look at the term *servant leadership* more closely and break it down into two action words, serving and leading. When we envision what serving and leading looks like in our minds, we get a picture of what servant leadership in action might look like.

As mentioned earlier, servant leadership is serving and leading simultaneously. It's important to understand that serving and leading at the same time is not a balancing act. Servant leaders do not determine when to lead and when to serve. It's a term that embodies the power of the *and.* Servant leadership is not leading or serving, it's leading and serving. Some hear the term servant leadership and process it like the term *work-life balance*, which is a paradox to living a life of purpose. In order to live a life of purpose and to lead with purpose, we must do away with the term work-life balance, and replace it with work-life integration. As we defined earlier, purpose is who we are and why we exist. It occupies all space and time in our lives, at work, at home, and anywhere else we may be. Similarly, servant leadership is an integrated term. You cannot fully be a servant leader and separate serving and leading into different time periods as if you are wearing two different hats at the same time.

One of the best works that I have read on the topic of servant leadership, which I consider an excellent resource, is *Servant Leadership in Action*. This book, edited by Ken Blanchard and Renee Broadwell, is a compilation of thoughts and perspectives by forty-two incredible authors and thought leaders on the topic of leadership in general. In the forward to this great work, John C. Maxwell said, "I get a kick when I hear people say that it's lonely at the top. To me, if it's lonely at the top, it means nobody is following you. If that's true, you'd better get off the top and go where the people are—and then, in my terms, bring them to the top with you."

What a powerful image. We cannot lead effectively, let alone lead with purpose, if no one is following us. If we are truly going to lead with purpose, we must have the heart of the servant leader, we must take our eyes off of ourselves and fix them on our purpose and on the people we are leading. As an African Proverb puts it,

"If you want to go fast, go alone; if you want to go far, go together."

I have been guilty of going too fast on too many occasions, and have found myself alone as a leader. Kurt David, my dear friend and co-founder of PurposePoint, often reminded me of this in the early stages of starting our organization. He would constantly say to me, "Remember it's better to move the whole team one foot at a time together, than to run ahead towards our purpose and vision alone. Look behind you."

This can be the challenge for visionary leaders. We quickly get a vision of what's possible, of what can be, and of what we can accomplish.

But in that excitement, we can fail to communicate our purpose, mission, vision, and values effectively and find ourselves off to the races with our team still looking for clarification at the starting line.

While I find it easy to keep my eyes fixed on our purpose, I am grateful to have a partner like Kurt who has pulled me back, time and time again, to make sure that I had them focused on our people as well.

The Servant Entrepreneur

"You get nothing, you lose, good day, sir!" I vividly remember the tone in which Gene Wilder's character said these words in *Willy Wonka and the Chocolate Factory*. As a child, I could not bear to watch this scene and often would walk up to the VCR and fast-forward right through it. Thirty years later, I found myself deeply resonating with his expression of frustration. In fact, I now believe this moment to be the most profound and meaningful scene in this original 1971 classic. Let me explain.

One of the most challenging tasks that leaders have is developing other leaders. One of the most difficult tasks entrepreneurs have is inspiring others to see their vision. But the hardest endeavor for both leaders and entrepreneurs is maintaining a servant heart. Having served in various leadership roles in my career, and now tasked with leading the vision of PurposePoint as an entrepreneur, I can personally state that this struggle is very real, but it is absolutely worth it.

Let's briefly walk through Wonka's struggle.

The premise of Willy Wonka's famous contest, to win a lifetime supply of chocolate, was merely a marketing campaign to find a successor for his factory. Wonka, played by the late Gene Wilder, targets a group of children to select a possible candidate to lead the future of his vision. Why children? In his own words, "Who can I trust to run the factory when I leave and take care of the Oompa Loompas for me? Not a grown up. A grown up would want to do everything his own way, not mine. So that's why I decided a long time ago that I had to find a child. A very honest, loving child, to whom I could tell all my most precious candy making secrets."

Wonka believed there to be an innocence in children that most of us lose in the pursuit of success. Unfortunately, there is also a selfishness that children and adults alike share that can derail the purest amongst us.

So, Wonka opens up his doors, opens up his tightly closed private life, and hopes that somewhere out there is a mirror of himself. We know how this plays out, as each child encounters the wonders of the marvelous factory, they fall into their natural self-serving desires, touching things they shouldn't touch and eating things they shouldn't eat, because they are only thinking of themselves.

One by one, Wonka's hopeful succession pool dwindles, and it seems for the moment that his efforts were futile. Even Charlie, who would seem to be the most innocent and selfless of them all, takes a fall. Wonka, with all hope now seeming lost, expresses his frustration with these famous words "You get nothing, you lose, good day, sir!" Charlie, who seems to not understand exactly what he did wrong, responds with an act of pure selflessness, and in that moment, Wonka redeems Charlie and finds his successor as he utters these words almost breathlessly, "So shines a good deed in a weary world."

We can get lost in the fantasy of films, but we can also find the very thing that is missing in this weary world and, if we actually apply it, it can become transformational. Many entrepreneurs and visionaries who have come and gone have been labeled as dreamers, and rightfully so. They see the unseen. They envision leaving the world a better place than what they were born into. They have a genuine heart to serve humanity with their thoughts, their ideas, and with their very lives. And, like Wonka, they look for the next generation to carry the torch, to carry their purpose.

History has been paved by entrepreneurs we memorialize, and also by those we mourn. I believe that the sole differentiating factor on which side of history they find themselves on is purpose. Every great thing that has ever been created, invented, or accomplished in this world started with a purpose. As long as that purpose remains noble, is not self-serving, and exists solely for the betterment of humanity, historical significance is inevitable. But as Wonka warns us, we live in a weary world, and like the many children he opened his factory up to, we can quickly lose sight of that purpose in pursuit of our own self-serving desires and end up on the wrong side of history.

Each of us has the potential to shape the future. You may be an entrepreneur, an employer, or an employee. Regardless of your title, role, or income, we all were created with a purpose that, if realized, will leave the world a better place than the one we were born into. We were meant for so much more, and we will only find it when we choose to lose ourselves in something bigger than ourselves.

CHAPTER 5:
AND NOW FOR PLAN A

I mentioned my friend Dennis Moseley-Williams earlier and his reference to "Taking the Great Leap." I first met Dennis in 2018 when I was invited by Dwight Eberts to a development seminar for financial advisors in Troy, Michigan. I had no idea who Dennis was or what he was going to be speaking about, but Dwight called me and insisted that I needed to meet him. Dwight and I have known each other for many years and have become very close friends ever since a mission trip to Guatemala that we were on together back in 2014. I have never met anyone who has a heart for people like Dwight. He is one of the most others–focused people I know. He is also one of the most purposeful people I know.

Later that week I showed up to Dwight's office, grabbed a coffee, and took my seat. A few moments later Dennis made his entrance, and the experience began. I use the term experience very intentionally. I sat there, mesmerized, for almost two hours as Dennis talked about the Experience Economy, challenging an audience of financial professionals on who they were helping their clients become. He captivated the room with his intellect, humor, and wit. And then he ended his presentation with this quote:

"The meaning of life is to find your gift. The purpose of life is to give it away." This quote has been attributed to both Pablo Picasso and William Shakespeare, but some believe that it originated from David Viscott.

I had heard all that I needed to hear. I was hooked. I was an instant Dennis Mosley-Williams fan. After Dennis's presentation I walked up, introduced myself, and applauded him on such an insightful, inspirational, and impactful talk. He was gracious and humble, genuine and refreshing. I could have sat and conversed with him for hours, or even just sat and listened for hours, but off to the airport he needed to be, so we exchanged contact information and off he went.

I could not sleep that night. Months before, our team at PurposePoint had started planning Purpose Summit 2019, and we were pretty much decided on the lineup and the agenda. While Dennis was not a member of our team, I just knew he had to speak at the Purpose Summit. He had captured the very essence of the conversation we were planning and had communicated it with such passion and clarity.

It should be noted that I had absolutely zero experience with putting together a summit of this kind, nor really did anyone on our team. We had many people on our team who were experienced at speaking at various events and hosting workshops and one-day seminars, but nothing of this magnitude. The idea behind the Purpose Summit was to invite individuals and organizations to come to a two-day experience that would serve as sort of a time out, to jump off the hamster wheel of life and day-to-day operations and refocus on who they are, why they exist, and what they were trying to accomplish—to realign with their purpose.

After meeting with our team, the following week I reached out to Dennis to invite him to speak at the Purpose Summit. He graciously agreed, and when the day of the summit came, he was absolutely transformational. Our entire team did such a fantastic job, as each of them mastered their own content and one-by-one impacted the lives of hundreds of people. I could have not been prouder of them, or more grateful for them.

Right after his talk, just as before, off to the airport he needed to be. But this time before he left, he paused and said these words. "Thank you so much for this. This was one of the most fascinating and memorable experiences that I have ever been a part of." A few hours later I received a text message from him that said this, "Sitting here on the plane still thinking about what just happened. Imagining what it would feel like to have been a part of the first-ever TED talk. What just happened is very special, and I am grateful to have been a part of it. Thank you for the opportunity."

Dennis returned home, and shortly after Purpose Summit 2019 recorded episode twenty-two of his blogcast series. The title of that talk was *And Now For Plan A*. Dennis recapped his experience at Purpose Summit 2019 and captured something that I had missed as we had been entrenched in the process of planning and executing the Summit: there was never a Plan B.

When you are clear about your purpose, of who you are, of why you exist, and the impact you were created to make on the lives of others, there can be no Plan B. Purpose is your Plan A. How you deliver that might evolve or change with time, your mission might change, your vision might change, but your purpose is finite.

Taking The Great Leap

Dennis and I continued to talk in the months that followed Purpose Summit 2019, and even spoke together at other events hosted by one of the organizations that came to the summit. During one of our phone conversations, I asked him what he was planning on speaking about at the next Purpose Summit.

He asked, "Have you ever heard of Billy Bragg?" I told him that I had not. He responded, "He's got this song called *Waiting for the Great Leap*. I've been captivated by the lyrics and asking myself why people wait for the great leap, some even wait so long that they never take it. I think that is going to be the title of my talk, *Taking the Great Leap*." When we think of taking a great leap, many people think about quitting their jobs, and for some that may be the case. That was the case for me. But I also want to be clear that you do not need to quit your job to find your purpose. It may mean exploring another role within your organization that is more aligned with your talents so that you can contribute at a greater level. It may simply mean showing up in your current role with a different perspective and attitude as you focus on how your job impacts others. Are your talents being utilized to their fullest? Are you contributing at the peak of your potential? What impact are you leaving on the table? What do you believe you are capable of? Dennis describes taking the great leap in its simplest form like this, "Taking the great leap is leaving everything you know for everything you believe." We all have beliefs about ourselves and our circumstances that limit us from the impact we are capable of making every day. The leap Dennis is referring to here is not a physical one, but a mental one. Self-limiting beliefs and fear are critical roadblocks that you must remove if you're going to fulfill your purpose. The fear of failing has prevented more people from achieving their purpose than anything else. Failure is inevitable. It is part of the journey. It's how we respond when we fail that makes the difference, as John C. Maxwell says. "Fail early, fail often, but always fail forward … The difference between average people and achieving people is their perception of and response to failure … If you're not failing, you're probably not moving forward."

You cannot play it safe and fully operate from a position of purpose. Life is going to hit hard no matter what position you take, but when those who operate from a position of purpose get knocked down, they get back up. There is no Plan B, there is only Plan A. The great philosopher Rocky Balboa put it this way,

"You, me, or nobody is gonna hit as hard as life. But it ain't about how hard you hit. It's about how hard you can get hit and keep moving forward; how much you can take and keep moving forward."

Living with purpose and leading with purpose requires us to keep moving forward, even in the most difficult of circumstances. I have often said, "Purpose is not just why we start, it's why we keep moving forward."

When you have a clear understanding of what your purpose is, of what you are called to do, and you believe it with every fiber of your being, your fears don't stand a chance. The self-limiting beliefs you once had fade in the rearview mirror of your journey like the skyline of a city as you depart from it. Everything that you once thought to be true that wasn't, everything you thought you knew about yourself changes, and it becomes easy to leave those thoughts behind for the purpose you now believe, toward the greater heights you are called to. As Brian Tracy said,

"You begin to fly when you let go of your self-limiting beliefs and allow your mind and aspirations to rise to great heights."

As I shared in chapter two, I took the biggest leap of faith in my professional career in May of 2016. The time since has taught me so much about others, and even more so about myself. It has been both reward-ing and challenging. There have been hills and valleys. There have been moments I have fallen, and others where I experienced what it feels like to fly, and here is what I have learned:

- When you have purpose and passion, the hills and valleys don't matter. Your purpose is level ground, and the rest is just per-ception. We often care too much about the judgments of others and their limiting beliefs that it makes us question our own self-worth and abilities. The voice of fear and the lies we tell ourselves derail us from achieving that which we are passion-ate about, that which we are called to do, and the life we were created to live. They leave us standing on the cliff of life looking out at the wide-open sky, asking ourselves *But just what if…*

- Be courageous. If you are looking forward to Friday and dread-ing Monday, it is time to take the great leap. Don't live another day not doing what you are great at and where people need you to do it most.

- Find your purpose and pursue it promptly and passionately.

- Believe in others and genuinely serve them. Be others–focused.

- Do not doubt your abilities or your capabilities. Raise the bar for yourself, rather than letting your fears and self-limiting beliefs set it for you.

- Challenge your mistakes, own them, but do not criticize yourself or blame others. Own it, learn from it, and move on.

- Seek feedback from those who believe in you and your potential, and make the adjustments that you need to right away.

- Try, fail, adjust, and try again. Fail forward. Fix your eyes on where you are going, not where you have been. The greatest achievement of all is not what you gain or accomplish for yourself, but who you become in the process, and who you help others become along the journey.

Finding Joy in the Journey

Have you ever met someone who is so overly optimistic in every interaction that it is almost too much to take in? It is as if they don't have a care in the world and are not living in the same reality as the rest of society? After all, everyone has something that they are dealing with, some challenge that they are facing, some weight on their shoulders, right?

It has been said that "You don't know what you have till it is gone." That is a popular phrase that needs no explanation, but only becomes of value and is understood when something is lost and, in most cases, those words don't offer comfort and happiness, but only perspective and regret.

I propose a different perspective: "Be thankful for what you have, that you once did not." Each one of us can look back at our lives and find a low point. For some of us that low point may be this very minute and, if so, these thoughts are even more so for you. If we pause, we can look at aspects of our current life that we can appreciate that once would not have been. Maybe it's your home, your health, your family, your friends, your faith … was there a time one of those items was a question mark or even nonexistent in your life?

At times, I have been described as the overly joyous, optimistic, carefree person I previously noted, and while some of you who know me and are reading this might agree, I would tell you that it is a daily choice for me to have that attitude, and it takes work.

I mentioned earlier in this chapter the mission trip that my friend Dwight and I went on some years ago. We had the privilege of visiting a small town in the remote hills of Huehuetenango, Guatemala, to spend a week building the foundation of a schoolhouse for the village, alongside village leaders and their families. I am often reminded of this trip, not by the mission work that we did, not by the breathtaking landscapes of mountains, volcanoes, waterfalls, or Mayan ruins, but by the simple smile of Kimberly. There in a town of tin and cement shacks, little work available, and many in need, lived this eight-year-old girl. Her bed was a small mattress on a dirt floor, shared with her younger brother, Alejandro. Next to it stood an old coffee table, which served them well for dinner each night, and next to that lay another mattress for her parents. Her father left each morning, hoping to find work that would provide provisions for the day, and her mother made hand-made tortillas and soup for their family, and for us, their guests. Kimberly and her brother helped out in any way that they could. And as we worked on our building project there each day, they were eager just to be a part of it.

In a field in the distance, there were kids their age playing with an old soccer ball, and while that fun called out to them, they found much more excitement in the bending of rebar for a pillar of their soon-to-be school and home. You see, the site we were building the schoolhouse on was once their home, and once the school building was completed, they would be able to build their home on top of it. They put the needs of the community before their very own as a family.

At the end of the first day we were there, Kimberly's father came home with a day's worth of wages. As he hugged his two little ones, he handed what he had earned to his bride, who then walked over to a lady on the road carrying a basket on her head. Kimberly's mom exchanged those wages for a basket of apples for us, their guests. A refreshing option I am sure she was thinking, from the soup and tortillas we had enjoyed while working long days in the sun. Kimberly walked over to the basket, grabbed an apple in her hand, walked toward me and, with the biggest smile I have ever seen, lifted it up and said, "Please enjoy!" They were a family of simple means, but they were the richest people I have ever met.

There is a piece of me that still lives in HueHue, and I believe it always will. But you don't have to travel to a third-world country to have an appreciative perspective on life. I can think back to a time when, like Kimberly, I was eight years old. I was living with my grandparents in a small row home in Philadelphia. They had five children, two of whom still lived there, and I lived in the basement, sleeping on an old-fashioned couch for four years of my childhood, while my parents were navigating the challenges of their divorce. I can still remember laying there at night—the familiar feel of the coarse fabric, the comforting smell of my grandmother's quilt, the aroma of her gravy (what we east coast Italians called sauce) always filling the air throughout this small, but warm home. I remember the simplicity, the innocence, and the kind of joy that Kimberly had in her smile, for I could see my eight-year-old self in her eyes. And while Kimberly had much less, she was much richer than I.

Time goes on, we grow old, life gets complicated. We fill it with endless to-do lists, we chase fleeting moments that bring glimpses of happiness, and we create and overreact to issues that in the end are of little significance. But if we pause … if we step away from the noise, we can rediscover the eight year old in all of us. We can reflect on the dreams of our childhood, of the great leaps we could take in this life, imagining what it would be like to spread our wings and fly. We can rediscover a joy that is rooted in our purpose. As C.S. Lewis stated in his book *Surprised by Joy*, "All Joy reminds. It is never a possession, always a desire for something longer ago or further away, or still 'about to be.'" What simple moments of joy in your past have you once forgotten that you can go back and live in right now?

What things in your life do you now have that you once did not?

What are you thankful for that each day you overlook?

What joy is lying dormant within you, that has yet to come out because you are waiting for something that seems further away or is about to be?

I encourage you today to stop waiting, to take that great leap in your mind. To use the talents, gifts, and skills you have been given to the fullest, and to experience joy in the process of doing so. You were created to specifically accomplish something on this earth, in this lifetime. It may be big or small, it could mean starting a worldwide movement, or simply mean being the best husband, wife, father, mother, leader, or colleague that you can be. Whatever your purpose may be, it is significant, for significance is not measured in size, it's measured in impact.

What impact are you making? What impact could you make?

There is no limit to the difference that you can make in this world, if you only choose to take the great leap from the limitations of safety and the busyness of chasing success into living a life of significance.

Know Your Why

We had just finished eating dinner and Vera, my daughter, who was eight years old at the time, turned to me and asked, "Dad, what is your job?"

Caught a little off guard, I simply said, "I'm kind of like a coach, kiddo, why do you ask?" She responded, "Just curious."

A few minutes later, she broke into a full impromptu interview. She said, "Dad, who do you coach?"

I said, "Mostly adults and businesses, like the stores we go to."

She said, "Ohhh, so you're kind of like a business coach?"

I said, "You could say that," surprised that she quickly pulled together that title.

She said, "Just one more question. Why do you do what you do?"

I said, "That is a really great question kiddo. I help people some-times see things they don't see so they can be better at what they do. We have all been called to do a job, and I think my job is to inspire others to do theirs the best they can."

She smiled, and said "Thank you, Daddy," and then walked into her coloring room. Little did she realize, she had just coached me.

We can get so caught up in who we are and what we do that we fail to remind ourselves consistently why we do it. I wasn't prepared for this profound interview by a second grader. The words that came out of my mouth in response to her simple questions were unfiltered and stripped of any language that would try to impress her. I found myself simply sharing with her what it is I do and why I do it, and she put together the rest.

Our son Bennett, who was five at the time, has learned from her. He became very inquisitive at a young age, and it seems that "Why" is his favorite question. I imagine that when he gets older, he is going to master the art of root-cause analysis, also known as asking the five whys. He has given me great practice in this area, particularly at eight-thirty at night, after tucking him in. In a last-ditch effort to procrastinate going to bed, each night he thinks of some question to ask followed by the question "Why?" many times.

This is a daily lesson we can each benefit from. Wherever you are right now, whatever you are doing this minute, I invite you to pause. Close your eyes and for just a moment imagine sitting with you eight-year-old self and ask yourself these questions:

- What did you do today?

- Who did you do it for?

- Why did you do it?

I recommend walking through this exercise each night before you tuck yourself in, perhaps keep a journal next to your bed. Pause, reflect on the day, and walk through these questions. You will find that doing so will keep you focused on your purpose in the good times and in the bad, and if you find yourself not being able to answer these questions, then you, my friend, might just have found yourself at the precipice of purpose, and it might be time to take the great leap.

CHAPTER 6:
PURPOSE, MISSION, WHY

I mentioned earlier on that the words purpose, mission, and why are often used interchangeably, and yet they each have their own very profound meaning. How you define and speak about these words each day shapes who you are, what you do, the impact you have on others, and your motivation each day to get up and move forward.

Over the years, I have come to define these terms this way, through how I have heard different thought leaders speak about them, and how I have seen individuals and organizations live these words out.

Purpose—Why you exist. Your reason for being.

Mission—How your purpose impacts the lives of others.

Why—What motivates you. Your reason for doing.

It is critically important for organizations to clearly define these terms so that the individuals within their workforce can effectively connect with their purpose at work. As an example, I'll share with you a story about my friend Jason Chise and his organization, OTR Performance.

Jason started OTR Performance initially as a diagnostic company. He had been a mechanic and had seen trucks coming into the shop all with the same problem. Jason thought to himself, *If this one truck driver is having this one problem, other truck drivers probably have this same problem.* He decided to find a solution to this problem. The end result was a diagnostic tool he developed in 2013 to address the issues these trucks were having while keeping them on the road, hence the name OTR. This was their purpose.

OTR's Purpose Statement: To create diagnostic tools that help keep trucks on the road.

What did this diagnostic tool mean for drivers? How did it impact them? It meant getting them to where they were going faster by equipping them with the power to perform diagnostics easier and faster than ever before.

OTR's Mission Statement: To equip you with the power to perform advanced diagnostics easier and faster than ever before.

I had the opportunity to interview Jason as the first guest on my first-ever podcast. He actually helped me name the podcast, and even had his technical team produce it. I had talked about the difference between purpose, mission, and why, and he said "That's what you should name it, people need to hear the difference between those terms and stories of those who are executing on them well." So we did. We later changed the name of the podcast to *The Finding Purpose Livec*ast, focusing on the stories of different organizations and their purpose. As I interviewed Jason, I asked him about OTR's why, and he told me a brief story of a thank-you letter that they had received. One of their customers was returning home from a long week of travel and was trying to make it home in time for Christmas when his truck broke down. Thanks to OTR's diagnostic tool, that driver was able to get home to his wife and kids to celebrate Christmas, which would have not happened if it wasn't for OTR executing on their mission. That story along with many others that followed became their why.

Since that time, OTR has not just developed multiple diagnostic tools, but they have expanded to develop other products, including a mobile application, all centered around the basic elements of their purpose and their mission, and driven by their why.

OTR's Purpose: To develop tools

OTR's Mission: To equip others

OTR's Why: To impact people

It is the simplicity and clarity of these statements that led to the success of Jason and his team, and the incredible growth of OTR. For any organization that wants to grow sustainably, the definitions of these words has to be clear and can never be compromised.

Where Talent Meets Purpose

Many organizations between 2008 and 2020 found themselves in uncharted territory. The average American under the age of thirty spent an average of just two years or less in a job. The workforce in general had seen a sharp decline in individuals staying in their role or with their company for a significant period of time, and even staying in the same industry. In the blink of an eye, job and employer loyalty fell from an expectancy of about fifteen years to five years to less than two years. How did such a dramatic shift happen in such a small period of time?

A generation that would transform the workplace as we knew it had entered the scene. As a society, we labeled them "Millennials." This was not an endearing term to them. If you think about it, the names that had been given to the generations before them had more purpose and meaning behind them. The Greatest Generation received their name due to their resilience during the Great Depression and World War II. Their inventions and innovations changed the way the whole world lived. Baby Boomers were named because of the mass increase of population that were born in the aftermath of WWII. Generation X came about partly because, in comparison to the generations before them, they were perceived to be disaffected and directionless, although some offer that they were named after Billy Idol's punk band that took its name from a book on youth culture published in 1965. Millennials were initially given their name as the generation being born into the new millennium (2000 AD). Although their name quickly took on a stereotype as a generation that was perceived as lazy and not hard working, the reality is that they were unmotivated because the currency of the workplace had shifted (more on the that currency shift in a moment).

As a result, many millennials left their jobs almost as soon as they started them. Finding young talent to stay became an epidemic that affected the workplace of every industry. This epidemic eventually reached beyond this newest addition to the working class. Eventually, the average lifespan of a job saw a dramatic downturn across multiple generations, including the Baby Boomers. It became known as the war for talent, as organizations competed at a level that they never had before to attract and retain their employees. Many organizations struggle with this same battle today:

- How do employees find fulfillment and consistency in their work that motivates them?

- How do companies attract talent that will stay and grow with them?

For organizations seeking talent, the answer is simple. It comes down to a culture of purpose. It is no longer enough to offer great compensation and benefits—those are only the cost of entry. To attract and retain great talent, you have to create an environment that makes your team jump out of bed in the morning, with no regard for the length of their commute, excited to step through those glass doors and into the arena, ready to make a difference.

Employers must be absolutely clear about what their purpose is, what their mission is, and the impact their people can make by being a part of it. They have to connect their why to their people's whys.

Employers, ask yourself these questions:

- Do we cast a clear vision of the impact we make as an organization and how each person on our team contributes to that?

- Do we provide an abundance of training, coaching, and support for the talent we brought on, and are we committed to their success?

- Is our team aligned on how we differentiate ourselves from the competition and the value we offer to our prospective clients, patients, or customers?

- Does our bottom line dictate the level of resources we provide to enable our team and, if so, is it limiting their potential, and ultimately our growth as an organization?

That said, ultimately the road back to stability in the workplace is owned by both parties.

Prospective job seekers, you must identify what you are good at, what the world needs, what you love, and determine the pay you need to earn for doing so. Then you need to find an organization that fuels that and hang on for more than just two years.

Talent seekers, in turn, you must create an environment that effectively communicates what impact you make, why candidates should come to work for you, how you will support them, and not allow the bottom line to compromise what you stand for. And you must commit to their development and growth.

This road may not be an easy one, but it is a necessary one. The success of both your career and your company is counting on it.

Talent Currency Shift

For generations, companies have had the luxury of a large talent pool, ripe for the picking. A phrase that I once was a proponent of, and have since backed off of, was "Right butts in the right seats." This is not a term that resonates with the incoming generation of leaders, nor with the next generation. If there is one thing that you should be well aware of by now, it's that people do not want to be treated as commodities; they never have, nor should they ever be. They don't want to be managed to a bottom-line goal for compensation; they want to be led to a purpose worthy of their time. This is not new information. Organizations have experimented with various terms over the years: team members, colleagues, partners, ambassadors ... you name it, anything to differentiate from the term *employee*. Why? Because they want to convey a sense of common purpose that they are striving for together.

The currency of the Greatest Generation and the Baby Boomers was their paycheck. They would do almost anything for overtime compensation, bonuses, or just to keep their jobs. The currency of the current and next generation is impact. It's no longer acceptable to simply use an engagement-friendly term that makes someone feel like they are part of a larger purpose. You have to create a tangible culture where colleagues actually experience impact directly correlated to their actions and alignment with your organization's mission.

Never before have we had such easy access to the transparency of a colleague's work history as we did when Linkedin became the main talent-discussion platform in the late 2010s. Likewise, never had we seen the honeymoon end so quickly. The average time an employee spent with an organization had drastically dropped from five years just a decade ago to eighteen months. Yes, eighteen months. A simple glance through your network showed not only how quickly individuals left companies but also how quickly they changed industries. People were not just leaving jobs, they were leaving the careers they thought they were pursing. Here is an illustration of the honeymoon curve.

We can attribute the lack of engagement and the negative impact to many things, but time and time again it often comes down to a misalignment of purpose.

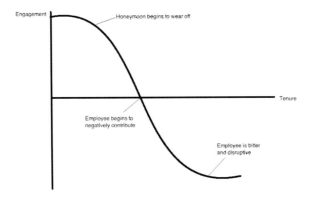

Engagement

Honeymoon begins to wear off

Tenure

Employee begins to
negatively contribute

Employee is bitter
and disruptive

This curve has existed through all generations. The difference is that the currency of the workplace has changed. Prior generations tolerated a misalignment and stuck it out for the long haul if it meant achieving that next pay raise, bonus, or promotion up the corporate ladder. Not so with the latter generations. They were looking for organizational purpose and alignment with their individual purpose and core values. Where prior generations were looking for a paycheck and perks, the next generation was looking for purpose and partnership.

Remember Jason Chise from OTR Performance? He was a millennial when he founded the company. He definitely did not fit the stereotype that society had placed on his generation. He was far from lazy and had a tremendous work ethic, and he hired other millennials who were just like him. The tremendous performance, rapid growth of his organization, and retention of his workforce had nothing to do with generational makeup and everything to do with operating with the right currency: purpose.

It should also be noted that purpose is not limited to corporate social responsibility (CSR). Too many organizations have jumped on the purpose bandwagon and commoditized that word by touting the way they are giving back to society. And while giving back and supporting our communities is a good thing, it can very quickly become a marketing tactic, and this should never be the case.

We don't lead with purpose because it is the popular thing to do or the profitable thing to do, but because it is the human thing to do.

In almost every talk that I have given, I have referenced the famous scene from the movie *The Big Kahuna* featuring Danny Devito. While I'm not a fan of the movie itself, there is a five-minute moment of brilliance in which Devito says these words, "If you want to talk to someone honestly, as a human being, ask him about his kids, find out what his dreams are, just to find out, for no other reason. Because as soon as you lay your hands on the conversation, to steer it, it's not a conversation anymore, it's a pitch. And you're not a human being, you're a marketing rep."

Organizations that effectively communicate their purpose and their mission, and connect their why to the why of their people, don't sell it. They live it out. Their purpose is not a pitch, it is a foundational element of who they are, of why they exist, and a guiding force behind all that they do. The character of any organization is tested the minute they prioritize profitability above their purpose. Yes, we must be profitable to operate. As it has been said, where there is no margin, there is no mission. Profit exists to serve the purpose, the organization, and its people, not the other way around.

Patrick Lencioni expands on this in his book *The Advantage: Why Organizational Health Trumps Everything Else in Business*. "Some executives, especially those who are a little cynical about all this purpose stuff, will say that their company exists simply to make money for owners and shareholders. That is almost never a purpose, but rather an important indicator of success, it's how an organization knows that it is fulfilling its purpose, but it falls short of providing the organization with a guide to what ultimately matters most."

The key to talent retention and sustainable growth is a healthy organizational purpose, a clear mission, and a motivating why. It requires us to refocus as leaders and individuals every day and ask ourselves what matters most, and to then align our thoughts and actions to that answer.

CHAPTER 7:
WHAT GOOD LOOKS LIKE

Refocusing on purpose can be unconventional in a world driven by performance and profitability. Perhaps one of the best examples of this organizationally is portrayed in the movie *Moneyball*. Based on a true story revolving around the 2001 Oakland Athletics, the plot gives us insight on developing a high-performing team by not focusing on high performers. In fact, Billy Beane, the Oakland A's general manager, loses all of his high performers to free agency and in self-initiated trades. On the surface, his strategy was viewed as insanity by the team's stakeholders, but Beane was focused on a purpose. He was focused on building a team that would win season after season. He was focused on growth, stability, and sustainability. His strategy—find players who were not performing to their potential—put them in the right position to leverage their strengths, and develop them as a team. Performance would ultimately follow.

I have had the opportunity to work for and with several organizations that have done this well. One such company is Costco Wholesale. It is hard not to like Costco. That giddy feeling of anticipation, of what's new, as you grab a cart, the smile and welcome of the greeter at the front entrance, the aroma of New York-style pizza in the air … it is more than a store, a club, or a warehouse, it is an experience. Unless you have ever had the opportunity to work there, even as a frequent member, you will miss what truly makes Costco special—its people, its purpose, and its founder.

I had the opportunity to meet Jim Sinegal, co-founder and CEO of Costco in 2001 when we opened a second wave of stores in the Michigan market. It seems like only yesterday that he reached out his welcoming hand with a sincere look, as if I was the only person in the room, and uttered the words "Hi, I'm Jim" from under his trademark mustache.

Since that time, I have worked with several organizations, both as an employee and as a consultant. In that time, I have come across various forms of engagement surveys, all aimed at asking the right questions to gauge and improve the culture of the workforce. It is widely known by now that engagement surveys are only as effective as what you do with the information you receive from them. Organizations spend millions of dollars each year on this effort, and often change up the surveys they use, looking for the one that will work magic. The reality is that the magic already exists within their organization, if they choose to invest time over money.

Jim, for all his brilliance and directness, embodied a simplicity and humility that was rare. His office, furnished with the same Lifetime table and chairs you saw on the floors of his stores, remained vacated most of the year. Jim had a personal mission to visit every one of his stores. As he walked each floor, he stopped, reach out his hand to his colleagues wearing the same name badge that he did, and warmly greeted them with "Hi, I'm Jim." He didn't stop there, he took the time to get to know who they were, why they enjoyed working at Costco, and what they felt could improve to make their warehouse better. He was a walking engagement survey.

If you ask those who experienced floor walks what that was like from a management perspective, they might recite the Five Rights of Merchandising to you: "The right product in the right place, at the right price, in the right quantity, at the right time." But from a leadership perspective, the most valuable lesson to be learned was what Jim exuded: The right person, with the right purpose, and the right passion, in the right position.

That is what made Jim a legendary founder and CEO. His purpose, which became the very mission of the organization, was simple:

- Obey the law

- Take care of our customers

- Take care of our employees

- Take care of our vendors

He would add, "If we do those four things right, we will achieve what every public company aims for, which is to reward our shareholders." Those words have never left me.

As I walk into the same store today that we opened back in 2001, nothing has seemed to change. It has taken on a whole new experience for me, for it is truly like taking a step back in time. The same cashiers behind the registers, the same representatives behind the membership desk, the same workers on the floor meticulously maintaining the building with pride and excellence as if it was opening day.

Where is the turnover? Where is the disengagement? Where are the generational gaps?

Leading a contagious culture that performs consistently at high levels does not have to be complicated or expensive. When you take the time to engage your core purpose as an organization, to inspire your people by making them feel a part of something greater than themselves, and you support them with the right processes and resources, performance follows.

Engagement is simply aligning with your purpose, your people, and your processes. It's not aligning them. Performance is merely an indicator of how well you do that.

People Over Process

We have talked a lot about placing purpose over profit, but equally important is honoring people over process. We can get so caught up in the assembly lines of our business processes that our people become a cog in that system. We forget that the system is designed to serve the people who are working toward the purpose our organizations exist for. CEO and co-founder of Menlo Innovations Richard Sheridan refers to this as "Eliminating human suffering" in his books *Chief Joy Officer* and J*oy, Inc: How We Built a Workplace People Love.*

Perhaps nowhere is this more evident than in the manufacturing industry. I am not immediately insinuating that all manufacturing organizations produce environments that lead to human suffering or labeling them as sweatshops, but for generations that has been the perception of the industry. And yet it is in this industry that I have found some very impactful examples of what good looks like.

One such organization is The Paslin Company, and I actually met Richard Sheridan through the CEO of Paslin, David Taylor. Since stepping into his role, Taylor has been on a mission to make Paslin, "The place in manufacturing where people want to work and where customers want to be," while learning from mentors like Rich Sheridan of Menlo Innovations.

Dave Taylor and I met in the C12 Group that I mentioned earlier. I did some consulting and leadership development work for his organization and eventually we became friends. I'll never forget the first leadership meeting I attended at Paslin.

"I've been at Paslin for just two months and I've been in this industry my whole life. I've never seen a culture of joy like this anywhere I have been in manufacturing." That was just one of the comments after an inspiring joint leadership session held by Taylor with every supervisor, manager, and executive on his team, the first-ever meeting of its kind.

"We cannot operate in a fear-based culture. We must trust each other as teams to say something when we see something wrong, regardless of role or title," said Taylor. He went on to say, "Each of you are leaders. You don't manage people. You manage tasks. You lead people to accomplish those tasks. Leaders don't meet people's wants, they meet their needs. It's my job to give you not what you want, but what you need."

In this statement, my friend Dave Taylor captures the essence of honoring people over process. It's giving them the process they need for them to achieve the purpose we are leading them to.

Another great example in this industry is L&L Products. I first learned of L&L Products when I was introduced to the president of their North America Division, Tom Kleino, through my friend Rick Venet who had also done some consulting work with Paslin.

L&L had more than a thousand employees in their workforce at the time, in multiple countries, with about half of them housed in their original Romeo, Michigan, location just twenty minutes from my house. Rick told me that I had to take a ride over there to meet Tom and experience what a fantastic culture he and his team were building. After Rick's kind introduction, I visited L&L Products and was captivated the moment I walked in the door. There on their wall were these words: "Our Purpose: To be a good place for all who touch it." This statement was everywhere, and it was more than just words on the wall, it was as if these words made up the very elements of the air that you breathed from the moment you walked inside.

As Tom, their president, and I walked their floor for hours, I was overwhelmed by the smiles on the faces of every employee I saw and the joy that filled every square foot of their facility. Tom knew everyone. And not just their name, he knew them, as a person, as a member of their family. Not since Jim Sinegal of Costco had I seen such a level of engagement of leadership. Story after story, employees shared how L&L had touched their lives, and Tom shared how each of those employees was touching the lives of others through their work. L&L had been known for the propriety adhesive they developed to hold and support manufactured products together. What I had found at L&L was that it was their purpose that was the adhesive that kept its culture together.

There are trailblazers changing the perception and the atmosphere of the manufacturing workplace, but L&L isn't one of them, they are the founders. They have been at this a very long time. Their culture is raw, real, and rooted in every fiber of their being. It truly is a good place for all who touch it, because they choose to honor people over process and lead with purpose in all that they do.

As I said in Chapter three with Lippert Components, the greatest product a company can produce is its culture. Just a few blocks from our office in Michigan is a small, family-run cabinetry company that makes same of the finest cabinets in some of the finest homes, not just in Michigan but in places like Martha's Vineyard. While their cabinets are exceptional, their culture is even more impressive. I had the opportunity to visit Bakes & Kropp in Mount Clemens, Michigan, and was overwhelmed by the contagious family atmosphere co-founder Paul Kropp, and his team, have created. From the moment I walked in the door, I could feel the engagement and commitment level of a workforce committed to something greater than themselves, and I was quickly introduced to the Bakes & Kropp way. Plastered on almost every wall throughout the factory are massive posters of the formula for their culture, with a central focus on safety and quality. The cornerstones of their formula focus on living out their values, maintaining a wow-factor workspace, working smarter and not harder, and identifying and eliminating waste.

Every Monday morning, Paul gathers his team for a one-hour weekly kick-off meeting. Not just the company leaders, every employee. During the first half of this weekly meeting, every employee shares a personal update about what is going on in their lives during that week. During the second half, they review the workload for the week ahead and align on production goals. The meeting then wraps up with a learning topic of the week, an investment in the personal and professional development of each and every employee.

Like many organizations, they consistently experience a heavy workload and every hour counts, yet they make time for this critical meeting every week without fail. In the meeting I attended, one of their employees announced the news of their soon-to-be first-born child, a potential future Bakes & Kropp employee. The employee making the announcement had been there just six years, and works there along with his father. You know a workplace culture is healthy when a six-year employee is already excited about having three generations of their family in your workforce. This is because the glue that holds their people together, their culture, is stronger than the glue that holds their cabinets together. They have incredible processes outlined in the Bakes & Kropp way, and those processes produce an incredible product: not just fine cabinets but a fine culture.

Organizations like Costco, Menlo Inovations, Paslin, L&L Products, Lippert Components, and Bakes & Kropp foster cultures that stand out because they consistently choose to focus on purpose and people more than they do processes and profit. They understand that as important as processes and profitability are to the sustainability of their organization, those items only exist to support the people who are driving their purpose forward.

Great leaders of organizations, such as these, continue to reinforce that purpose by constantly engaging their teams, by consistently seeking feedback from them, by giving them not what they necessarily want, but what they need to achieve their purpose. They get to know their people, really know them, who they are, their stories, their individual why for coming to work every day. They invest in their development to help them achieve both their individual purpose and the organization's purpose. And most importantly, great leaders recognize their people, not just for their contributions to the organization or to the team, but for their individual accomplishments as well. They cheer their people on to achieve the purpose they were created for.

Balcony People

In her book *Balcony People*, Joyce Landorf Heatherly describes such people as those who are in the balcony of your life, cheering you on. One of the greatest examples of this that I have come across in the workplace is the people at Broad River Retail, an independent licensee of Ashley HomeStores, led by CEO Charlie Malouf. Charlie is the embodiment of recognition. He and I met each other though LinkedIn, as his continual posts celebrating his people caught my attention. Howard Shultz, former CEO of Starbucks used to consistently say, "We are not a coffee company that serves people. We are a people company that serves coffee." This is true of the people in Charlie's organization, who call themselves

"Memory Makers." They are not a furniture company that sells to people. They are not even a people company that sells furniture. They are a "people company that makes memories by selling furniture." This is the core of their purpose statement: "Furnishing Life's Best Memories." The Memory Makers at Broad River Retail are not there to close the sale, they are there to celebrate the moment. They have become balcony people for their customers and for each other, and Charlie is not in some higher balcony above them by himself cheering his people on. He is right beside them, on the same level, giving them high fives. Each time a team member hits a sales milestone, it is a celebratory moment. Not because of the dollar mark they achieved, but because of what that dollar amount represents: impact.

Charlie and his team believe that purpose begins with identity. It is rooted in who they are. Charlie became president and CEO in 2015, and purchased controlling interest in the company in 2018. One of the first things he did after taking the reins was to build a foundation upon clarity of purpose:

- Who was Broad River Retail?

- What did they want to be known for?

- What was their identity?

They created diagrams as a team and took apart their previous mission statement word by word, connecting the work that they do to the impact they create for their customers. They restructured employee levels, titles, and compensation based on milestones and impact, and in 2019 launched their Year of Purpose. In August of that year they held their very own internal purpose summit, specifically on the date August 28, which they called Purpose 8:28. Even the name and the date they chose were purposeful, giving a nod to Romans 8:28. As a team, they recognized they were created for a greater purpose, and that they were in this together. On that date, leaders from different Ashley HomeStore locations came together to share their identity, to celebrate each other and their purpose as an organization.

The times when we need to be in each other's balconies most are in the hardest of times. It hasn't always been all sunshine and rainbows for Charlie and his team at Broad River Retail. They have been through some tough times, as we all have. But it was their purpose and their unity as a people that enabled them to persevere through those times. Perseverance reveals character. It's in our most challenging times that we find what we are made of, where we reveal our true identity, and when we often see what good truly looks like.

CHAPTER 8:
WE ARE ALL IN THIS TOGETHER

The year 2020 may forever be remembered as the year the world came to a screeching halt due to the coronavirus or COVID-19 pandemic. But I believe that history books will record 2020 as a year when we didn't just talk about purpose, we chose to live it out, together.

Millions of people across the world were infected, and hundreds of thousands died during this terrible time, and yet in the midst of this tragedy, never had we seen such solidarity, compassion, support, and collaboration rise up across the globe.

It was truly an unprecedented time. Dozens of countries ordered national shutdowns. Schools were closed, government offices were closed, businesses that were considered non-essential to the support of life were closed. Hundreds of millions of people were out of work, hospitals across the nation and the world were at capacity, military tent hospitals were being built in parks across the country to make room for the thousands of sick that traditional hospitals did not have room to care for. And in the midst of all of this, leaders of some of the largest companies in the world gathered daily with government leaders in our nation's capital to collaborate on what purpose they and their teams could serve in humanity's greatest time of need.

Automotive manufacturers who halted production of vehicles and closed their plants said, "We can retrofit our factories and make ventilators where we were making cars starting next week, and try to save as many lives as we can."

Clothing manufacturers said, "We will sit at our sewing machines for hours a day, sewing masks and caps for doctors, nurses, and home health care workers to keep them alive so they can continue to save lives."

Household goods manufacturers and spirit distilleries said, "We can transform our facilities and focus our efforts on producing sanitizers, disinfectants, and even work on creating a possible vaccine."

Diagnostic companies came together and collaborated to invent testing for the virus that yielded results in a manner of minutes when just a month prior those same results would have taken a week to get back.

And it wasn't just big business and corporations that stepped up, the humanitarian effort on a local level was equally impressive.

Restaurants who were closed to the public said, "We have kitchens and staff, and will continue to prepare food for take out or delivery to feed families who are out of food due to empty grocery store shelves and support parents who don't have time to make dinner because they have been teaching their kids in their homes all day."

Teachers said, "We will support parents virtually from our living rooms, helping them to teach their children. We will do online lessons and do all we can to help children finish the school year from home."

Moms said, "We will share our blogs and activity ideas with one another to support each other and our children. Let's make the most of this opportunity while we must stay at home with our kids."

Celebrities said, "We will read books to your children and sing songs on live feeds to encourage the hundreds of millions who are sheltered in their homes."

Nurses and doctors worked tirelessly, serving back-to-back shifts, many of them wearing the same masks they had already worn for days because there were not enough masks to go around, each of them putting themselves at risk to help the infected, many of them living in separate tents or in their garages, not being able to see their spouses and kids, in an effort to protect their families.

Social media feeds were filled with videos of medical professionals standing on the roofs of hospitals, praying, praising, and worshiping in the middle of their greatest storm. Days later, additional videos emerged of those same hospitals parking lots filled with cars flashing their hazard lights in a show of support for those brave heroes on the front lines of this battle.

On a global scale, the best of humanity was taking center stage in the midst of a worldwide pandemic. More viral videos emerged on the scene of neighbors in Italy singing to each other form the confines of their balconies, where about twelve percent of the infected population was dying. Soon similar videos followed from Spain, France, and other countries. Scenes from across the world showed us buildings with their room lights flashing throughout them, signaling support like the hazard lights in the hospital parking lots, as people inside them flicked on and off their light switches.

Countries who months prior were exchanging adversarial rhetoric were suddenly sending desperately needed resources to each other, despite whatever the status of their relationship was prior to this crisis. Throughout all of this humanity cried out one loud, unified, purposeful message: "We are all in this together."

The original title of this chapter was supposed to be Finding Purpose in a Pandemic, but I felt that this phrase, one that became the resounding anthem of mankind during this time, was much more purposeful. A serendipitous change, for shortly after I wrote these very words, another friend and colleague of mine, Zach Mercurio Ph.D., wrote an article entitled "Finding Purpose in a Pandemic." I reached out to him and asked if I could share some of his words here, and he agreed. And so here are the words of my friend Zach written on March 17, 2020, in the midst of the pandemic.

Finding Purpose in a Pandemic
by Zach Mercurio

I was in the parking lot at my kids' daycare when I got the notification. I looked down at my phone, and nausea returned. The first word of the e-mail subject line read, "Canceled." It was the latest in a string of messages that obliterated my false sense of stability, security, and purpose.

A big part of my work comes from sharing research through speaking to large groups. It's not a very pandemic-resistant occupation. A few months of work was wiped out on a Friday afternoon. I'm one of the lucky ones. I don't live paycheck-to-paycheck. I don't face food insecurity. I don't rely on a front-line service job for my family's health benefits. Still, I felt an eerie emptiness. Why? The true value of something in our lives is often revealed when we lose it.

It's always a risky bet to tie our identity to what we do. At some point—because of a pandemic or some other external inevitability—we won't be able to do it. Then what? When the thing disappears, our sense of self goes with it.

For many of us over the next few weeks and months, the activities we thought gave our lives meaning will change or vanish. Parents won't have the bustle of bringing kids to and from school, rehearsals, and practices. We won't be able to go to our regular church service, to our weekly happy hour with friends, or take our favorite workout class. Remote workers won't get to see their co-workers or their customers every day, and many artists and athletes won't get to practice crafts they've spent their whole lives honing. We've been forced to pause, quarantined to reflect.

In this newfound vacuum of activity, we have an opportunity to move on to better questions, ones that we know result in longer-term thriving: Apart from what I do, achieve, or produce, who am I? Why am I? What is my purpose in the absence of all the doing?

It's first essential to realize that your purpose isn't what you do, it's the contribution you make through what you do. School, a job, or a volunteer position are all ways through which you make an impact, not the impact itself. Realizing this difference is powerful, because as soon as you can separate what you do with the impact you want to make, new possibilities emerge that aren't confined to a role or activity (that you may not be able to do anymore). Purposeful people tend to focus more on the contribution they can make where they are, and not on the things they do.

A few years ago, my ninety-seven-year-old grandfather sent me a card for my birthday. In it, he asked one question: "How do you improve the moment?" That is the question for this moment. The one constant on even our worst day is the opportunity to contribute.

Zach Mercurio, Ph.D., is a purposeful leadership and meaningful work researcher, professor, strategist, speaker, and bestselling author of The Invisible Leader: Transform Your Life, Work, and Organization with the Power of Authentic Purpose.

* * *

What Zach outlined here is exactly what individuals and organizations around the world started doing almost overnight. In our worst of days, humanity looked for opportunities to contribute.

The original meaning behind the title of this book, *Finding Purpose at Work*, was intended to help individuals and organizations reconnect with the purpose of what they do in their work. But as I take stock and process the unfolding moments of 2020, the phrase "Finding purpose at work" takes on a whole new meaning, one where purpose takes on a persona and work becomes a verb. If we pause and look closely, we can see purpose at work, in some way in every area of our lives. The way that we live purposefully and lead with purpose in every moment is to align our thoughts and actions with what purpose is doing in the moment. You may have different beliefs or ways of describing this supernatural alignment. For me, it's walking in the spirit—seeking and discerning what God is doing in the moment and aligning my thoughts and actions to His. Whatever your belief, there is evidence all around us that we are all a part of something greater than ourselves, a greater purpose that we have a natural instinct to contribute to. We were created for community, to serve each other with our gifts, talents, abilities, and resources. Anything we gain from doing so is a mere byproduct of living out our purpose.

As Patrick Lencioni said in his book, *The Advantage*, "All organizations exist to make people's lives better … Every organization must contribute in some way to a better world for some group of people, because if it doesn't, it will, and should, go out of business."

Even as I write these words, despite historical relief stimulus measures that have been taken to keep businesses in business—covering the costs of payroll, rent, and other operational expenses—businesses are closing permanently. It will become increasingly clear in years to come that the businesses that survived this time did so because they found a way to contribute to the moment, they were more focused on their purpose than they were concerned about profit.

There is an old story that paints a picture of a group of people gathered in a room, each with a long spoon attached to their arm, too long to reach their mouths. At the center of the room is a table with a large bowl of food—an ample amount to feed all. One version of the story ends with the narrative that since they cannot feed themselves, they all starve.

Another version of the story embraces the power of their humanity in the moment—they learn how to feed each other using what they each have been given.

It shouldn't take a crisis or a pandemic to unleash the power of humanity. Even in the best of times, we must learn to pass the spoon. We are all in this together.

CHAPTER 9:
ONE CUP AT A TIME

If there's one thing that people know about me, it's that I love coffee. I am not ashamed to admit that I have a borderline coffee problem. It's rare that I'm not walking around with a cup in my hand. The thing is, I really don't need it. Caffeine has little effect on me, and while I love the taste of a good, bold dark roast, it is the actual comfort of a cup in my hand that is the hard habit to break.

The only thing that makes coffee better is when it is shared with others. Some of us get so busy in this life trying to make a grandiose impact, while others get caught up in trying to make a name for themselves. Both are endless pursuits that never slow down, and can only truly be measured when we stop to take a sip from the cup of life and taste what we have been brewing.

I recently had a coffee meeting with a former colleague of mine who had been asking me to get coffee for months. I remember the first time I met him in 2010, when I was appointed as his new district manager, and he, thirty years my senior, mumbled the words, "What does this kid think he is going to teach us?" under his breath. For the years we worked together, I respected his years of experience and knowledge, while he tolerated my persistent feedback to try and make him a better leader. We weren't kidding ourselves, we both knew that the only thing he really wanted was for me to not visit him and to leave him alone to run his business. Each visit was the same, the two of us with cups of coffee in our hands, reviewing his business and going back and forth in what seemed to always be a circular conversation.

Years have passed since I left that retail world and he retired. Our lives went in significantly different directions, mine becoming much busier, while his became much less. As I continued to focus on the future, it became harder and harder to stop and take that sip of life with an old friend. He called me out on it, and I'm glad that he did.

As we came together to share stories of the old, laughing in affirmation of the thoughts that were going on in our minds back in those days, he shared something I did not see coming. Bringing the coffee cup up to his grey mustache, and then setting it back down, he looked at me and said "I can think of three leaders in my career that I learned something from, the first two taught me a lot about business, but you taught me a lot about people. You helped me become a better person." That was a good cup of coffee, one that I will forever be grateful for, and humbled by.

An hour later on the same day, I found myself sitting in another coffee shop, in another meeting, but this time with a new friend. A few months earlier we had met at an HR conference that PurposePoint had sponsored. Her company's table was just a few short steps from ours, and I could not help but notice that both of our organizations played in the same sandbox. I introduced myself and listened as she shared her passion for coaching and consulting, which had spanned more than two decades. Interestingly, we were both scheduled to deliver keynote talks with similar titles on winning the war for talent, both taking place in the same week in the same community. Now I try to see everything through the lens of collaboration and not competition but, in full transparency, this was a challenge for me. I thought long and hard about the situation, and out of respect for her tenured experience, I decided to change my title, and even attended her talk. For that hour, I sat and listened as she shared stories of those in her past who helped her become who she was today, and how she used their stories to transform the lives of others. She was real. She was authentic. She was refreshing. After her talk, I shared my commentary during the post video session in appreciation for her presentation.

One month later, I received a request from her to have lunch. Not knowing what to expect, I agreed and listened intently as she shared her stories of triumphs, failures, and her current struggles. There was no agenda, just a genuine introduction of two like-minded professionals in the same field. After two hours of conversation, our meal ended, and we went our separate ways.

Two weeks later, I received an email from her that I will never forget. For me that lunch seemed to be just another introductory lunch, but for her it was a transformational experience. Here she was on a mission to discover her purpose, even though she had been changing the lives of others for decades.

Both of these individuals taught me something.

- You never know who might be learning from you and how you might be impacting their life, no matter how old you or they may be.

- It is never too late to discover your purpose, regardless of what you have or have not accomplished in your life.

Maybe there is such a thing as too much coffee, maybe there isn't. What is important is not how much you have, but that you stop to taste each sip. In every moment of life, there is an opportunity for you to impact the lives of those around you, even if you are not looking for it. And so, in this ever-increasingly fast-paced world, I urge you to stop and take a sip, to experience the fullness of living a life of purpose, and to taste each moment—one cup at a time.

Be a Bob

Each year, my family and I cherish time together watching the beloved classic *White Christmas*. We cozy up by the fire with a large bowl of popcorn for the kids, and two hot cups of coffee for Amy and I. Before I can press play, there is usually a conflict between brother and sister over who has more popcorn and a larger section of the blanket. There are givers in this world, and there are takers.

- Takers. We are born creatures of habit and have a natural inclination toward the instinct of survival. Focusing on one's own needs with little regard to the needs of others can lead to a level of selfishness that can only be reversed by brokenness. But there are some who develop a natural instinct for wanting to help others with no regard to the impact to themselves.

- Givers. One of my favorite scenes in *White Christmas* is when Bob Wallace, a very others–focused individual, finds a unique opportunity to express a simple form of gratitude to Major General Waverly. The retired General receives an anticipated letter in which he was hoping to reestablish his sense of self-worth by assuming a position back in the Army, only to find he is passively rejected. Having built a successful career as an entertainer with his partner Phil Davis, Bob gets an idea to lift the General's spirits, leveraging his own resources with no expense spared, and with no desire for personal gain.

A few years back I had the opportunity to meet with a different Bob, a well-accomplished innovator and product developer who works with several large household brands. My dear friend Joe Sciacchitano introduced me to Bob Moesta, founder of The Re-wired Group. As the three of us sat in Bob's cozy, well-furnished office—a unique setting void of any surfaces—each enjoying our respective choice of caffeinated beverage, something extraordinary occurred.

You see, I came into this meeting fully expecting that there was some way I was supposed to help Bob. I assumed Bob came into this meeting thinking there was some way he was supposed to help Joe, and Joe came into his meeting thinking there was some way he could help both Bob and I. Three givers. There we sat for two hours, discussing the current state of society, the marketplace, barriers, thought process, and solutions. Bob, being a gracious host, remained fully others–focused and shared several insights that created a paradigm shift for me, one that led to the launch of PurposePoint. I learned much about Bob, and not because he shared so much about himself, but because he shared so much of his self.

I had many meetings that week, but I could not stop thinking about this one. While the content of the discussion was highly valuable, that is not what had captivated me. It was the environment that was created by three innovative thinkers with an others–focused mindset, coming together for a genuine conversation and leaving titles, accomplishments, and any self-serving agendas outside the room.

A few years later I had a similar encounter with another Bob, my now good friend Tim Turczyn, president and CEO of TeleRegen, Inc. Our mutual friend Al Beahn introduced Tim and I. We had lunch one day at a restaurant just outside of my office in Mount Clemens, Michigan, which is an important detail. Our lunch location was a walk across the street for me, while it was over an hour drive across town for Tim. But that's the kind of person Tim was, as I quickly learned. He was not concerned about meeting in the middle, he was focused on the purpose of the meeting and opportunities to make a greater impact together. The cost to himself was of no consequence. Tim walked into that lunch with a stack of files of his most recent purposeful endeavors. A lunch that was supposed to be one hour turned into three, and we never got to those files. He was enamored with the work that we were doing at PurposePoint, and every time I tried to shift the conversation back to his work, he said "Keep going, I'm more interested in what you have to say." In the weeks that followed I received a call from Tim with an introduction to someone "I just had to meet" almost every week. Tim was constantly looking for opportunities to help people and connect people who wanted to help people, to make a difference with people who wanted to make a difference.

"I want to make a difference, with people who want to make a difference, doing something that makes a difference.
— John C. Maxwell

There is such power in collaboration when people are focused on purpose. My friend Tina Marie Wohlfield is another Bob. I first met Tina, of course over a cup of coffee, after an introduction on LinkedIn. Tina is the embodiment of collaboration. In fact, the name of her book is *Stop, Collaborate, and Listen*. These words are more than just a book title, or lyrics from a 1990s song. They are a mental formula. So many people listen to respond, but not Tina. She listens to collaborate. In every interaction she listens, and subconsciously is thinking, *Who does this person need to know? Who can I introduce them to? How can I help?*

- What can happen when we park our egos, skepticism, and self-serving ambitions at the front door?

- What can happen when we re-evaluate who we are focused on and how we communicate?

- What if in your next interaction you share less about yourself and more of yourself?

I believe progress in this world is made by givers, people who welcome conversation, ideas, and dialogue, without skepticism, focusing on what they can contribute. Sadly, these moments of opportunity are passed by too often, met with self-focused responses of "I'm too busy" because we are so focused on our own agendas, or if we do take the time, we are focused on our own return on investment (ROI) for that time.

In the movie *White Christmas*, there is a line that gets a bad rap, "Great little angle, isn't it?" Everyone always seems to have an angle.

What if, like Bob Wallace, that angle was not self-serving? What if there were more givers and fewer takers?

What if the next time someone asked or offered to meet with you, your focus was on what you might be able to contribute to the meeting, and not what your agenda or your ROI could be?

What if that meeting changed not only their life or yours, but countless others?

What could we accomplish if we approached every moment like the Bobs I just spoke about?

Imagine the possibilities of a society in which everyone chose to stop, collaborate, and listen in every conversation.

We all have the opportunity to be givers, but it requires us to take our eyes consistently off of ourselves and place them on others, even in our most challenging times and moments of brokenness.

Broken for a New Purpose

"What was that?" she screamed from the living room. "Was that the special cup I bought for Daddy?" A brief pause, and then a river of tears, followed by uncontrollable sobs from our then six-year-old daughter poured forth. I had just walked into the other room when I heard the crash. I knew something had fallen in the kitchen and had certainly broken into a million pieces, as my bride was putting dishes away. Before I could arrive on the scene, I was made aware by a little heart-broken voice of what just happened.

Two weeks earlier, our six-year-old daughter, Vera, went to school filled with anticipation and a twenty-dollar bill in her hand, her heart full of joy and the excitement of going to her first Santa shop at school to buy presents for her mommy, her daddy, and her little brother. She came home that day even more excited with three carefully wrapped bags and said, "Now don't look! I am going to place these under the tree, and Daddy, here is your change!" Tears of joy came to me at the sound of these words. She had been so happy and responsible with what we had given her, and now her precious gift was broken.

I sat in the other room, pondering how I was going to try to heal her heart, and somehow replace what was now broken. After all, we could just go buy a new coffee cup. Secretly this idea appealed to me, as I am not much of a comic guy, and the cup she so proudly gave me had a large batman symbol on it with the word Dad across it, but it was from her heart, and I'll never forget her words and her smile when I opened it. "It has a batman on it and says Dad, because you are my super Daddy." Heart. Melt.

So, as I held back the words, "We will just go buy a new one," I surveyed the scene, and then without effectively even seeing if it was possible, said, "Vera you like puzzles! How would you like to help Daddy put the cup back together?"

The sobbing came to a halt, and slowly a grin from cheek to cheek appeared, and she responded, "That's a great idea, I will get the tape!" and to the drawer she ran! I, however, staring at the floor and seeing the largest remaining piece to work with was about the size of a silver dollar, had just realized that I may have over promised. But there we sat, piece by piece, mending, smiling, laughing, restoring. What once was broken, now mended, and whole.

You can still see the cracks, the tape, and even a few chips that were beyond repair. The cup, once used to sip coffee from, could no longer be used for its basic function. It no longer has a place in the cabinet with the other coffee cups, mixed in and hidden, unless selected for use. It has now been set apart by itself, and has become so much more. What once may have been packed away as the years went by, or even donated—by accident of course—now has a permanent place on my desk and in my heart. I may have spent years drinking coffee from it, and not once remembered any of those moments, no matter how many hundreds of times I may have used it. But this is for certain: I will never forget the hour Vera and I spent putting it so very carefully back together. Piece by piece, we created something much more than a memento, we created a moment, and one I shall never forget.

We each are created for a purpose, and for many, they go through life just serving their basic design, blending in with the others, a life filled with moments just as fleeting as the sips from an ordinary coffee cup. There are moments in life when the unexpected happens and, sometimes, those unexpected events shatter us. How do we respond?

I could have simply said, "Let's buy a new cup," swept up all of the broken pieces, threw them in the trash, and moved on. I could have been so focused on the important stuff going on in our busy day and not taken the time to think about my daughter's heart, and how to respond in this unexpected moment. What a tragedy that would have been, for I would have lost so much more than just a cup had I done so.

So, how do we respond when the unexpected happens? What would we miss out on, if we just tried to pass those moments by, cover up the pain, and move on?

What were you created for? Are you going through life living out the basic functions of a human being? Blending in? Just another cup in the cupboard? Or perhaps you are made to be broken. Even the most beautiful flowers and trees we have seen start as a single seed, and that seed must be broken to become what it was created to be.

Maybe you are reading this and you feel just as broken as the cup I described. Even in the darkest of times, as I described in the final chapter of this book, a purpose can be found, and when you find it, that purpose can restore you, piece by piece, into someone capable of so much more than you were before.

Maybe you are so busy in this life trying to make some grandiose impact, or caught up in trying to make a name for yourself, that you miss engaging in the truly important moments that are meant to shape you. I have found purpose at work most in my life in the moments that I am forced to take a pause, and perhaps it may be time for you to do just that.

A Collision with Purpose

"You're a bad driver." Those were the words our daughter, Vera, screamed out of her passenger window at a lady whose name I may never know. It was a normal day driving Vera to school, and we were singing our favorite song together, smiling, laughing, enjoying our simple morning routine. As I approached her school, which also happens to be our church, I put my left-hand turn signal on and stopped to wait for the oncoming traffic to pass. I looked back at Vera, smiling, singing, and watched the upcoming car behind us pass around us and, instantaneously, the laughing turned to screaming.

The car behind the car that passed us slammed into us at fifty miles per hour. The back of our SUV was crushed all the way to Vera's car seat. Gas started pouring out, and my tank indicator immediately dropped to empty. All I could think about was getting my daughter out of her car seat, and out of the car. But I could barely move. The sound of the crash was so loud that those inside our church heard it and thankfully were on the scene immediately to pull both Vera and I safely out of the vehicle.

I still hear the crash in my head, the screams of my daughter, and can see the inside of what was left of our car, as well as the devastation to the car that hit us. I do not know what happened to the other driver, other than that she also was taken to the hospital that day. I only pray that she is well. For me this was a forced moment of pause.

We take our lives for granted, living in the fast lane of busyness, routine, and procrastination. We suppress our potential to fulfill the purpose we were created for, telling ourselves "Tomorrow ... Someday ... One day."

But we are not promised tomorrow. We are not promised someday. We are not promised one day. We are only promised today.

As I laid in the hospital bed with my neck in a brace, directed to be completely still, and very much uncertain of what my future held, I took stock of what truly mattered. I committed in that moment that if I were blessed to be able to walk again, that I would walk with purpose, making each day and every moment count in this life. I committed that if I were blessed to run again, that I would run the race that was set out before me, not procrastinating a moment longer because I was too busy or stuck in the routine of my comfort zone.

I committed that if I were blessed to speak again, that I would speak into the lives of others, devoted to fulfilling my purpose by helping others find theirs. Thankfully, by the grace of God, I did. I walked out of that hospital, and I set out to live my life purposefully from that moment on.

Envision what this would look like if each person lived out their purpose fully. Envision what your life would look like. Many of us confuse busyness with performance and, as a result, we never reach our full potential, and often find ourselves living lives of indifference. There are some who know their potential and their purpose, but are not living in it, and as a result are living lives of frustration. And there are others who don't see their potential or their purpose, are not living in it, and as result experience depression.

Purpose = Joy

This may be the most simplistic and underutilized equation in all of human history. When we focus on our purpose, we fulfill our potential and experience high performance in all that we do, and we experience joy in all that we do. When we choose to lead with purpose, we empower others to do the same. Here is a basic diagram that I drew on piece of copy paper one day to illustrate this point.

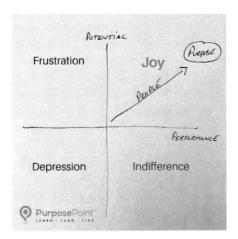

We are all on a collision course with life, with purpose, and, ultimately, with death. The road we take matters to those whose lives we collide with while we are here, and to those who will come long after we are gone.

CHAPTER 10:
"YOU GOT A GIFT"

In memory of Daniel P. Marsh

"You … You … You got a gift my friend. You got a gift." These words spoken by Robert De Niro's character in the 1999 hit movie *Analyze This* will forever echo in my mind through the voice of my dear, late friend Daniel Marsh.

I first met Dan at a Starbucks by our home in 2017. I was having coffee with my friend Jim, who also happened to be a colleague of mine at the time, and we were discussing takeaways from a Bible study we had recently started together. We were sitting at a long community table that seats about ten people, yet we were the only three sitting there. Dan was at the far end of the table with papers strewn all around him. It turned out that Dan was a very busy attorney and those papers were his case notes. As my friend Jim and I were talking, Dan looked over, and in his bold intimidating voice abruptly interrupted and said, "Are you guys talking about Jesus?"

I responded, "Actually, yes we are."

Dan said, "Man, I love Jesus, what are you guys talking about?" And so Dan joined the conversation.

There we sat, Jim and I with our new friend Dan for about an hour. As we wrapped up the conversation, I asked Dan, "Have you ever heard of the C12 Group?" (As I mentioned earlier, the C12 Group is a national Christian peer advisory group for CEOs and business owners). He responded that he had, and our conversation went something like this:

He said, "C12, C12 … You mean Roger Norberg?"

I said, "Yep, that's the one. Have you considered checking it out?"

He said, "I met Roger ten years ago, but I didn't think it was for me when we talked back then. Do you think that C12 stuff is worth it?"

I said, "Dan, I met Roger two years ago and I didn't think it was for me either, until I recently visited a group. I wish I could go back and put my pride and ego in check and had joined sooner. I've met some incredible CEOs and business leaders in the last few months that are truly building great businesses for a greater purpose."

He said, "Maybe I'll give Roger a call and check it out."

The next month, I stepped into our monthly C12 gathering and there sitting at the table was a new familiar face, Dan Marsh.

Dan became more than a member, he became an ambassador for the group, and every person in it. That was the type of person he was. If he believed in something or someone, he was all in. He became the biggest advocate for those he believed in.

Dan and I became great friends. Over the next two years, Dan, Roger, and I met for breakfast almost every Friday morning to discuss opportunities to introduce more purpose-driven leaders in the Detroit market to each other, and to extend an invitation to those who were so inclined to join us around the C12 table. Dan had a gift for connecting people. He had an uncanny ability to maintain a library of information in his mind, and pull from it at any moment to give people the resources they needed faster than they could explain their problem to him. It was as if he was an intellectual doctor, walking about society, listening to the symptoms of those all around him, friends and strangers alike, and jumping into any conversation with an immediate prescription. Like a doctor said, "Here, take two of these and call me in the morning," I can hear him now saying, "Here, read this book, or call this person, and let me know how I can help."

Dan was one of the most others–focused, purpose-driven individuals I have ever met, and he was one of my biggest encouragers. At almost every breakfast we had together, he held onto something that I said in that conversation, and say to me, "You … You have a gift. People need to hear what you are saying." He encouraged me to start speaking on a larger scale, he prompted me to launch PurposePoint, and he spurred me on to write this book. I am forever grateful that God placed him in my life. He constantly challenged me, which helped me take steps in my life that brought me closer to the person I was created to be.

Dan challenged everyone around him, and he may have had no filter, but he had great conviction. One of my greatest memories of Dan was when we were looking at available space to expand our office in Mount Clemens, Michigan, to include a co-working space for other purpose-driven entities. Dan had planned to move his legal office into our new co-working space and serve as an in-house attorney for our members. The new space we were looking at was directly across the street from the county courthouse, which Dan frequented several times a week as an attorney. As we were looking at the different offices and the views outside of those offices, Dan immediately went to the office that overlooked the courthouse and said, "This is it. This is my office. I have to have this office. Now I can look straight at that courthouse and keep those judges in my sight each day, and pray for them and the cases they are presiding over." Everything he did and every decision he made was purpose centered.

Dan never had the opportunity to pray in that office. At our Friday breakfast the week after we stood in that office, he received a phone call. It was from his doctor. His tone changed in a manner I had not heard before. He closed his books, looked up calmly at Roger and me, and said, "Boys, I have to go. My doctor just called and told me to come in right away because they need to look at something." I had no idea he was sick, and he would have you believe that he didn't know he was sick either, but I believe he knew. He was not one to share his burdens, because he was always so focused on relieving the burdens of others. He could see the look of concern and panic on my face. He stood up, put his arm on my shoulder, gave me his Dan Marsh smile, and said, "I'm gonna be okay."

Even in his moment of greatest need, he was concerned about my burden for him. That was the last time that I saw my friend Dan.

In the following days, Dan was admitted to the hospital, and he and I texted back and forth almost every day as I attempted to encourage him as he so often encouraged me. Encouragement was a spiritual gift that I believe we both shared and was the foundation for our friendship, second only to our shared faith. Even from his hospital bed, Dan was still digesting information and sending it out to those who needed it. We were in the midst of the COVID-19 pandemic, and the hospital he was in was overwhelmed with patients. Each day my inbox filled with messages and articles with resources for business leaders on what they needed to know to lead their teams in the midst of COVID-19, and many of them were emails from Dan.

Dan operated from the center of his purpose right to the very end. He used his gifts of knowledge, wisdom, and encouragement to serve others, even during his darkest moment. He ran the good race and he fought the good fight. Micah chapter six, verse eight (NIV) reads, "He has shown you, O mortal, what is good. And what does the Lord require of you? To act justly and to love mercy and to walk humbly with your God." Dan's life exemplified these words.

I shared in the beginning of this book that this is not intended to be a religious work, and my intent is not to disengage you in this moment if you do not share the same beliefs that Dan and I shared, but I cannot refrain from sharing scripture here as I am compelled by the last words I received from my friend Dan. His last words to me were, "He has not moved away. I do need to get into the Word more. I have found much comfort there." Within thirty-six hours of these words, he had gone to be with the Author of the Word.

Romans chapter twelve, verse six (NIV) says, "We have different gifts, according to the grace given to us. If your gift is prophesying, then prophesy in accordance with your faith; if it is serving, then serve; if it is teaching, then teach; if it is to encourage, than give encouragement; if it is giving, then give generously; if it is to lead, do it diligently; if it is to show mercy, do it cheerfully."

"You … You … You got a Gift."

Your life itself is a gift. You have been created for a purpose, that somewhere, someone needs you to operate in the fullness of. At the end of the day, our lives are measured in impact. The greatest measure of purpose is who we help others become. I pray that the words in this book help you to not only find your purpose at work, but to find purpose at work in your life. I pray that you would realize the incredible potential that is within you to make a difference in this world, and that like Dan, your purpose will impact the lives of all those it touches, and perhaps even end up on the pages of some book, long after you are gone.

ABOUT THE AUTHOR

Davin Salvagno is the founder and CEO of PurposePoint and a keynote speaker known for connecting purpose, people, and performance. Having spent nearly two decades serving in various leadership roles in finance, human resources, operations, and marketing with Fortune 500 companies, his insights and talks have helped hundreds of organizations across the world engage their purpose, inspire their people, and positively impact their performance. He also serves as a corporate consultant, helping organizations clearly define their mission, vision, and values, and is a subject matter expert on multi-generational shifts, talent attraction, engagement, retention, and social communications. Davin currently resides in Michigan with his wife, Amy, and their two children..

Learn more at www.DavinSalvagno.com